Mediterranean Diet Cookbook for Beginners

2000+ Days of Easy, Tasty & Nutritious Recipes for Lifelong Health | Full Color Pictures, No-Stress 30-Day Meal Plan & Shopping List for Effortless, Balanced Eating Every Day.

Madison Mitchell

TABLE OF CONTENT

INTRODUCTION

In today's world, it feels almost impossible to prioritize our health and well-being, especially when it comes to what we eat. Quick and convenient options are everywhere, making it all too easy to settle for processed and unhealthy meals. But while these foods might satisfy our immediate hunger, they often leave us feeling unfulfilled.

Our unhealthy eating habits and sedentary lifestyle have increased the risk of cancer, diabetes, cardiovascular diseases, obesity, and other diseases. As our health declines, our life expectancy has greatly decreased as well. We sacrifice both our wellbeing and forget to nourish our bodies. Only when we are faced with our declining health or eminent mortality do we realize that we should have taken good care of our bodies.

Well, it's not too late to change even though many people are searching for a way to break this cycle. This is where the Mediterranean way of eating comes in. The diet can help you achieve that desired health you need physical and mentally. It is a unique approach that will definitely turn your life around three hundred and sixty degrees.

Mediterranean diet is a lifestyle that celebrates the simplicity and wholesomeness of fresh, seasonal ingredients. For centuries, people from Mediterranean regions have thrived on meals rich in vegetables, fruits, whole grains, lean proteins, and healthy fats like olive oil. These dishes are not just delicious but have been proven to promote longevity, heart health, and a balanced life.

But the problem many face is knowing how to incorporate this way of eating into their own daily routines. With so much information out there about diets and healthy eating, it's easy to feel overwhelmed. How do you get started? What do you need? Can this approach really fit into your lifestyle?

In this cookbook, you'll discover that eating the Mediterranean way is not only possible but also deeply satisfying. Each chapter is filled with simple, delicious recipes that will help you embrace this way of cooking—without the stress of complex techniques or obscure ingredients. It doesn't matter if you're a Pro, or a beginner, the recipes are designed to fit seamlessly into your lifestyle, offering both nourishment and full of flavor.

By the time you've worked your way through these chapters, you'll have a new outlook on food. You'll see how easy it can be to prepare meals that are packed with nutrition. You'll feel more energetic, more satisfied after eating, and perhaps most importantly, more connected to the food you eat. And you don't have to be an expert to achieve this transformation.

What inspire this book is that I have spent years exploring the rich culinary traditions of Mediterranean countries, not just as a chef but as someone deeply passionate about the life-enhancing benefits. After experiencing firsthand how these meals can bring vitality and balance into daily life, I was motivated to share that knowledge with the world. This isn't just about following a set of rules but to enjoy delicious food in a way that's sustainable for both your body and your lifestyle.

Obviously, the Mediterranean diet is far from dull. To follow the diet effectively, all you need is to know more about the diet and it range of health benefits. There is so much to discover about Mediterranean food! Do yourself a great deal to follow through the pages, so as to help yourself improve your eating habits.

THE MEDITERRANEAN DIET

The Mediterranean diet isn't something new. Far from it. Its roots go deep into the past, tracing back to the eating habits of ancient civilizations. The diet is the traditional dishes of nations bordering the Mediterranean Sea, such as France, Spain, Greece, and Italy. It is a balance of foods rich in antioxidants and healthy fats, and high in fiber. Also, the diet focuses on spending time with loved ones while preparing and enjoying meals, self-control, exercising, and reducing stress. That is where the lifestyle part comes in, caring for all aspects of your life as a whole.

Although the Mediterranean diet is a modern nutritional recommendation, this eating habit is as old as the civilizations that thrived on the banks of the Nile River, the Mediterranean region where the ancient yet advanced civilizations arose. Along with the progress of history, the customs, cultures, religions, languages, thinking, and lifestyle of the Mediterranean region also flourished. The diverse cultures integrated with one another and the eating habits merged.

However, the actual origins of the Mediterranean diet are lost in time. The passing of history has made various developments and changes in the eating habits of the people in the Mediterranean region. Despite this, the importance of vegetables as the major component of the Mediterranean traditional foods was retained.

The diverse historical path, the geographical traditions and connotations that characterizes the eating habits of the countries in the Mediterranean region, and the difference between the current diet and the Mediterranean diet of our ancestors, and the introduction of the new food has given us the Mediterranean diet, as we know it today.

The modern Mediterranean diet is a healthy and nutritious eating model or plan that is closely related to the original historical, territorial, environmental, cultural, and social Mediterranean lifestyle throughout history.

Presently, the Mediterranean enhances the safety and the quality of food. This eating habit offers simple cuisine, but is rich in taste and imagination, taking advantage of all the aspects of a healthy diet. It is an eating choice that preserves the customs and the traditions of the Mediterranean region eating habits.

THE MEDITERRANEAN DIET PYRAMID

The Mediterranean Diet Pyramid is a visual representation of the recommended food groups and proportions in the Mediterranean Diet. It serves as a guide to help individuals understand the balance and distribution of different food categories within this dietary pattern.

At the base of the Mediterranean Diet Pyramid are physical activity and social connections, highlighting the importance of an active lifestyle and the enjoyment of meals in the company of others. Moving up the pyramid, the following food groups are represented:

Plant-Based Foods: Fruits, vegetables, whole grains, legumes, nuts, and seeds form the foundation of the Mediterranean Diet. These foods are rich in vitamins, minerals, fiber, and antioxidants. They are recommended to be consumed in abundance, providing the body with essential nutrients and promoting overall health.

Olive Oil: Olive oil is the primary source of fat in the Mediterranean Diet and is considered a healthy alternative to other cooking oils. It is used for cooking, dressing salads, and flavoring various dishes. Olive oil contains monounsaturated fats and antioxidants, which have been linked to numerous health benefits.

Dairy Products and Fish: Dairy products, such as yogurt and cheese, are consumed in moderation in the Mediterranean Diet. Fish and seafood, particularly fatty fish like salmon and sardines, are also included due to their omega-3 fatty acid content, which is beneficial for heart health.

Poultry, Eggs, and Sweets: Poultry, eggs, and sweets are to be consumed in moderation. These foods are not central to the Mediterranean Diet but can be enjoyed occasionally.

Red Meat and Sweets: Red meat and sweets are placed at the top of the pyramid and are recommended to be consumed sparingly. These foods are not considered essential in the Mediterranean Diet and are limited due to their potential negative impact on health.

The Pyramid provides a visual representation of the proportions and frequency of different food groups, emphasizing the importance of a plant-based diet with limited consumption of animal products and processed foods. It encourages individuals to prioritize whole, unprocessed foods that are rich in nutrients and to enjoy meals mindfully, savoring the flavors and experiences that come with this balanced way of eating.

HEALTHY BENEFITS

In my findings, I discovered that people whose diet comprised mostly of vegetables, fruits, grains, beans, and fish were among the healthiest. Thus, if healthy living is your desire, it will be helpful to get a look at the big picture. I have studied the characteristics of the Mediterranean diet for years now and the following evidences support the healthfulness of the Mediterranean diet.

Healthy and long life: The Mediterranean cuisine is often referred to as the healthiest cuisine in the world and the diet doesn't stray too far away.

Being based mostly on fresh vegetables and fruits, healthy oils and whole grains, as well as lean meat and seafood, it's not hard to see why this diet is considered this healthy. Combine it with a glass of red wine and you've got yourself a fun, easy going diet.

Heart Health: Scientific evidence easily connects a good heart health with certain foods, mainly vegetables, fruits, olive oil and nuts. And the Mediterranean diet has it all!

Weight Loss: Although the main focus of this diet is not weight loss, it will surely help with it if that's what you're looking for. Just look at it from this point of view: fresh, clean food combined with whole grains, good fats, less sugar and plenty of liquids and exercise. You have all the ingredients for an evident weight loss.

Controls Diabetes: Because it focuses on fresh ingredients and it packs plenty of vitamins, antioxidants and minerals, this diet is a great way to keep your diabetes under control.

Retaining your mobility: Muscle weakness and other signs of frailty are reduced by 70% in the elderly who follow a Mediterranean diet.

No risks involved: The Mediterranean diet is one of the most balanced diets, therefore there are no risks involved as long as you eat everything with moderation, do plenty of exercise and drink as much liquids as you can.

It is affordable: The Mediterranean diet is accessible even if you're on a budget. Beans, vegetables, fruits, herbs and whole grains as well as a good quality olive oil are not as expensive as they sound, but they offer so many cooking options.

Increasing Life Expectancy: Those who follow a Mediterranean diet have a 20% lower risk of developing heart disease or cancer and a 20% lower overall mortality rate.

Cardiovascular Disease and Stroke Prevention: Reducing the amount of refined bread, processed foods, and red meat you eat, as well as encouraging the use of red wine instead of hard liquor, are all things you can do to help prevent heart disease and stroke.

So, if you've been searching for a way to eat better, feel better, and live better, this book is here to guide you. An experience that will transform not only the way you cook but the way you think about food altogether. And where better to begin this transformation than with the most important meal of the day—breakfast? In the next chapter, you'll explore how Mediterranean-inspired food can set the tone for your day, providing you with the energy and nourishment needed.

Let's begin.

GET YOUR BONUS

30-Day Meal Plan

Complete Shopping List

Recipe Index

US and Metric Measurement Units

CHAPTER 1: BREAKFAST

Oatmeal with Apple and Cardamom

Ingredients

- 1 tbsp. light olive oil
- 1 large Granny Smith apple, peeled, cored, and diced
- ½ tsp. ground cardamom
- 1 cup steel-cut oats
- 3 cups water
- ¼ cup maple syrup
- ½ tsp. salt

Time: 17 min. Servings: 4 Calories: 249

Directions

Sauté the oil in the Instant Pot. Add apple and cardamom and cook for 2 min. Press Cancel. Add oats, water, maple syrup, salt, and stir. Close lid, set to Sealing, press Manual, and cook for 5 min. When it beeps, release pressure naturally for 10 min, then quick-release until the float valve drops. Serve hot.

Nuts and Fruit Oatmeal

Ingredients

- 1 cup rolled oats
- 1¼ cups water
- ¼ cup orange juice
- 1 medium pear, peeled, cored, and cubed
- ¼ cup dried cherries
- ¼ cup chopped walnuts
- 1 tbsp. honey
- ¼ tsp. ground ginger
- ¼ tsp. ground cinnamon
- ⅛ tsp. salt

Time: 17 min. Servings: 2 Calories: 362

Directions

Place oats, water, orange juice, pear, cherries, walnuts, honey, ginger, cinnamon, and salt in the Instant Pot. Stir to combine. Close lid, set to Sealing, press the Manual, and cook for 7 min. When it beeps, release pressure for 20 min. Press the Cancel button, open lid, and stir well. Serve warm.

Breakfast Hash

Ingredients

- Olive oil spray
- 3 potatoes, diced
- ½ yellow onion, diced
- 1 green bell pepper, seeded and diced
- 2 tbsp. olive oil
- 2 tsp. granulated garlic
- 1 tsp. salt
- ½ tsp. freshly ground black pepper

Time: 40 min. Servings: 6 Calories: 133

Directions

Line the air fryer basket with parchment and spray with oil. In a bowl, mix the potatoes, onion, bell pepper, and oil. Add the garlic, salt, and pepper and stir until coated. Transfer the mix to the prepared basket. Air fry at 400°F for 20-30 min., shaking or stirring every 10 min., until crispy.

Greek Deviled Eggs

Ingredients

- 4 hardboiled eggs
- 2 tbsp. Roasted Garlic Aioli
- ½ cup crumbled feta cheese
- 8 pitted Kalamata olives
- 2 tbsp. chopped sun-dried tomatoes
- 1 tbsp. minced red onion
- ½ tsp. dried dill
- ¼ tsp. ground black pepper

Time: 30 min. Servings: 4 Calories: 147

Directions

Slice the eggs in half lengthwise, remove the yolks, and place the yolks in a bowl. Reserve the egg white halves. Smash the yolks well with a fork. Add the aioli, feta, olives, sun-dried tomatoes, onion, dill, and pepper and stir to combine until smooth and creamy. Spoon the filling into each egg white half and chill for 30 minutes, covered.

Mashed Chickpea, Feta, and Avocado Toast

Ingredients

Time: 10 min. Servings: 4 Calories: 301

- 1 (15-oz.) can chickpeas, drained and rinsed
- 1 avocado, pitted
- ½ cup diced feta cheese (about 2 oz.)
- 2 tsp. freshly squeezed lemon juice or 1 tablespoon orange juice
- ½ tsp. freshly ground black pepper
- 4 pieces' multigrain toast
- 2 tsp. honey

Directions

Put the chickpeas in a bowl. Scoop the avocado flesh into the bowl. With a masher, mash the ingredients until the mix has a spreadable consistency. Add the feta, lemon juice, and pepper, and mix. Evenly divide the mash onto the four pieces of toast and spread. Drizzle with honey and serve.

Overnight Berry Muesli

Ingredients

Time: 8 hr. Servings: 4 Calories: 220

- 1 cup of muesli
- 2 cups of mixed frozen berries
- 2 cups of plain kefir

Directions

Divide the muesli between four Mason or similar jars. Add a half-cup of kefir on top and then a half-cup of berries. Stir to combine, put the lid on, and refrigerate overnight. This can be left in the fridge for up to four days. Stir well before you serve it.

Garlic Scrambled Eggs with Basil

Ingredients

- 4 large eggs
- 2 tbsp. chopped basil
- 2 tbsp. grated Swiss cheese
- 1 tbsp. cream
- 1 tbsp. olive oil
- 2 cloves garlic, minced
- Sea salt and freshly ground pepper, to taste

Time: 10 min.	Servings: 2	Calories: 267

Directions

In a bowl, beat the eggs, basil, cheese, and cream with a whisk until combined. Heat the oil in a non-stick skillet over medium-low heat. Add the garlic and cook for 1 min. Pour the egg mix into the skillet. Work the eggs continuously and cook until soft. Season with salt and pepper to taste. Divide between 2 plates and serve immediately.

Quinoa with Figs and Walnuts

Ingredients

- $1\frac{1}{2}$ cups quinoa, rinsed and drained
- $2\frac{1}{2}$ cups water
- 1 cup almond milk
- 2 tbsp. honey
- 1 teaspoon vanilla extract
- $\frac{1}{2}$ teaspoon ground cinnamon
- $\frac{1}{4}$ teaspoon salt
- $\frac{1}{2}$ cup plain Greek yogurt
- 8 fresh figs, quartered
- 1 cup chopped toasted walnuts

Time: 22 min.	Servings: 4	Calories: 413

Directions

Place quinoa, water, almond milk, honey, vanilla, cinnamon, and salt in the Instant Pot. Stir to combine. Close lid, set steam release to Sealing, press the Rice button, and set time to 12 min. When it beeps, let pressure release naturally, about 20 min. Press the Cancel button, open lid, and fluff quinoa with a fork. Serve warm with yogurt, figs, and walnuts.

Walnut Poached Eggs

Ingredients

- 2 slices whole grain bread toasted
- 1 oz. dried tomato, sliced
- 1 tbsp. cream cheese
- 1/3 tsp. minced garlic
- 2 slices prosciutto
- 2 eggs
- 1 tbsp. walnuts
- ½ cup fresh basil
- 1 oz. Parmesan, grated
- 3 tbsp. olive oil
- ¼ tsp. ground black pepper
- 1 cup water

Time: 20 min. Servings: 2 Calories: 317

Directions

Pour water in a pan and boil. Then crack eggs in the boiling water and cook for 3-4 min. Meanwhile, churn the minced garlic and cream cheese. Spread the bread with the cheese mixt. Top with dried tomatoes. Add pepper, Parmesan, oil, and basil to the mix. Transfer the poached eggs over the dried tomatoes and sprinkle with pesto sauce. Serve hot.

Creamy Breakfast Bulgur with Berries

Ingredients

- ½ cup medium bulgur wheat
- 1 cup water
- Pinch sea salt
- ¼ cup almond milk
- 1 tsp. pure vanilla extract
- ¼ tsp. ground cinnamon
- 1 cup fresh berries of your choice

Time: 10 min. Servings: 2 Calories: 173

Directions

Put the bulgur in a medium saucepan with the water and sea salt, and bring to a boil. Cover, remove from heat, and let stand for 10 min. until water is absorbed. Stir in the milk, vanilla, and cinnamon until fully incorporated. Divide between 2 bowls and top with the fresh berries to serve.

Spinach Omelet

Ingredients

- 2 eggs
- 1 cup torn baby spinach leaves
- 1 ½ ounces grated Parmesan cheese
- A pinch of onion powder
- A pinch of ground nutmeg
- Salt and pepper to taste

Time: 15 min. | Servings: 1 | Calories: 186

Directions

Beat eggs in a bowl, then stir in spinach, Parmesan, onion powder, nutmeg, salt, and pepper. Heat a small skillet over medium heat, spray with cooking spray, and pour in the egg mixture. Cook for 3 minutes until partially set, flip with a spatula, and cook for another 2-3 minutes. Lower heat, cook for another 2-3 minutes until done. Serve warm and enjoy!

Feta, Spinach, and Red Pepper Muffins

Ingredients

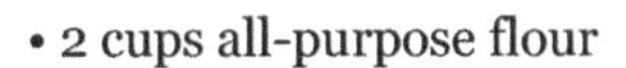

- 2 cups all-purpose flour
- ¾ cup whole-wheat flour
- ¼ cup granulated sugar
- 2 tsp. baking powder
- 1 tsp. paprika
- ¾ tsp. salt
- ½ cup extra virgin olive oil
- 2 eggs
- ¾ cup low-fat 2% milk
- ¾ cup crumbled feta
- 1¼ cups spinach, thinly sliced
- ⅓ cup red peppers, chopped

Time: 32 min. | Servings: 4 | Calories: 243

Directions

Preheat the oven to 375°F and line a muffin pan with 12 liners. In a bowl, combine the flour, wheat flour, sugar, baking powder, paprika, and salt. In another, whisk the oil, eggs, and milk. Add the wet to the dry ingredients, and mix. Add feta, spinach, and peppers, and mix. Divide among the liners. Bake for 25 min. Set aside for 10 min, and remove from the pan.

Mediterranean Frittata

Ingredients

Time: 25 min. | Servings: 2 | Calories: 520

- 4 large eggs
- 2 tbsp. fresh chopped herbs (rosemary, thyme, or oregano)
- 1 tsp. dried herbs
- ¼ tsp. salt
- Freshly ground black pepper
- 4 tbsp. olive oil, divided
- 1 cup spinach
- 4 ounces quartered artichoke hearts, dried
- 8 tomatoes, halved
- ½ cup crumbled feta cheese

Directions

Preheat the oven to low broil. In a bowl, whisk together eggs, herbs, salt, and pepper. Heat 2 tbsp. olive oil in a pan over medium heat, sauté spinach, artichokes, and tomatoes for 1 to 2 min. Pour in the eggs mix, cook for 3-4 min, and sprinkle with cheese. Broil for 4-5 minutes until set. invert onto a plate, slice, and drizzle with remaining olive oil. Serve warm.

Italian Breakfast Bruschetta

Ingredients

Time: 30 min. | Servings: 4 | Calories: 305

- ¼ tsp. kosher or sea salt
- 6 cups broccoli rabe, chopped
- 1 tbsp. olive oil
- 2 garlic cloves, minced
- 1 oz. prosciutto
- ¼ tsp. crushed red pepper
- Nonstock cooking spray
- 3 large eggs
- 1 tbsp. 2% milk
- ¼ tsp. ground black pepper
- 4 tsp. Parmesan cheese
- 1 garlic clove, halved
- 8 slices baguette bread

Directions

Bring a large stockpot of water to a boil. Add salt and broccoli, boil for 2 min, then drain. Heat oil in a skillet over medium heat, add garlic, prosciutto, and red pepper flakes, cooking for 2 min. Add broccoli and cook for 3 more min. Whisk eggs, milk, and pepper. Scramble eggs in the skillet, then mix in broccoli rabe and cheese. Toast bread, rub with garlic, and top with the egg mix. Serve.

CHAPTER 2: BEANS, GRAINS AND PASTA

Quinoa with Artichokes

Ingredients

- 2 tbsp. light olive oil
- 1 yellow onion, diced
- 2 garlic, peeled and minced
- ½ tsp. salt
- ½ tsp. ground black pepper
- 1 cup quinoa, rinsed
- 2 cups vegetable broth
- 1 cup chopped marinated artichoke hearts
- ½ cup sliced green olives
- ½ cup minced parsley
- 2 tbsp. lemon juice

Time: 36 min. Servings: 4 Calories: 270

Directions

Sauté oil in the Instant Pot. Add onion and cook for 5 min. Add garlic, salt, and pepper, cook for 30 sec. Press Cancel. Stir in quinoa and broth. Close lid, set to Sealing, press Manual, cook for 20 min. When it beeps, release pressure naturally, for 20 min, open lid. Fluff with a fork, stir in remaining ingredients. Serve immediately.

Rice Soup

Ingredients

- 3 cups chicken stock
- ½ lb. chicken breast, shredded
- 1 tbsp. chives, chopped
- 1 egg, whisked
- ½ white onion, diced
- 1 bell pepper, chopped
- 1 tbsp. olive oil
- ¼ cup brown rice
- ½ tsp. salt
- 1 tbsp. fresh cilantro, chopped

Time: 30 min. Servings: 4 Calories: 176

Directions

Pour oil in the stock pan and heat. Add onion and pepper. Roast for 3-4 min. Add rice and stir. Cook for 3 min over medium heat. Add stock and stir. Add salt and boil. Add chicken, cilantro, and chives. Add egg and stir carefully. Close the lid and simmer for 5 min over the medium heat. Once done, Serve.

Brown Rice with Zucchini and Tomatoes

Ingredients

- 1 cup brown basmati rice
- 1¼ cups vegetable broth
- 5 tbsp. olive oil, divided
- 2 cups chopped zucchini
- 2 cups sliced cherry tomatoes
- ¼ cup minced red onion
- 2 tbsp. lemon juice
- ¼ tsp. salt
- ¼ tsp. ground black pepper
- ¼ cup chopped parsley
- ¼ cup toasted almonds
- ¼ cup crumbled feta cheese

Time: 27 min.	Servings: 6	Calories: 209

Directions

Place rice, broth, and 1 tbsp. olive oil in the Instant Pot, stir, and set to Manual for 22 min. After cooking, release pressure naturally for 10 min, then quick-release. Fluff the rice, transfer to a bowl, and cool. Add zucchini, tomatoes, and onion. Whisk remaining olive oil, lemon juice, salt, and pepper, then pour over the rice and toss. Top with parsley, almonds, and feta. Serve warm.

Cumin Quinoa Pilaf

Ingredients

- 2 tablespoons extra virgin olive oil
- 2 cloves garlic, minced
- 3 cups water
- 2 cups quinoa, rinsed
- 2 teaspoons ground cumin
- 2 teaspoons turmeric
- Salt, to taste
- 1 handful parsley, chopped

Time: 25 min.	Servings: 4	Calories: 384

Directions

preheat the Instant Pot. Add the oil and garlic, stir and cook for 1 min. Add water, quinoa, cumin, turmeric, and salt, and stir. Lock the lid. Select the Manual and cook for 1 min on high. When it beeps, perform a natural release for 10 min, then release what left. Remove the lid. Fluff the quinoa with a fork. Season with salt, if needed. Sprinkle parsley on top and serve. .

Brown Rice and Beans

Ingredients

Time: 35 min. Servings: 4 Calories: 350

- 1 cup brown rice
- 2 cups vegetable broth
- 15 oz. black beans, rinsed
- 1 large onion, chopped
- 2 cloves garlic, minced
- 1 red bell pepper, diced
- 1 tsp. smoked paprika
- ½ tsp. cumin
- ¼ tsp. cayenne pepper
- Salt and pepper to taste
- 2 tbsp. olive oil
- Parsley for garnish

Directions

Heat olive oil in a skillet over medium heat. Sauté onion and garlic until translucent. Add bell pepper; cook for 2 min. Add brown rice; toast for 1 min, and stir. Pour in the vegetable broth and bring to a boil. Reduce heat to low, cover, and simmer for 20 min. Stir in beans, paprika, cumin, cayenne, salt, and pepper. Cook for 5 min. Serve with parsley.

Bean and Olive Tapenade

Ingredients

Time: 10 min. Servings: 4 Calories: 150

- 1 cup cooked white beans (cannellini or navy)
- ½ cup pitted Kalamata olives
- 2 tablespoons capers, rinsed
- 2 cloves garlic, minced
- 2 tablespoons olive oil
- 1 tablespoon lemon juice
- Salt and pepper to taste
- Fresh parsley, chopped (for garnish)

Directions

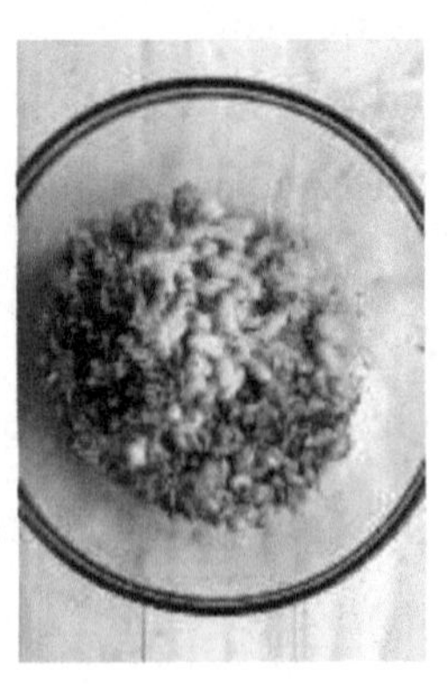

In a food processor, combine the white beans, olives, capers, and garlic. Pulse until the ingredients are coarsely chopped. With the processor running, slowly add the olive oil and lemon juice until the mixture becomes a coarse paste. Season with salt and pepper to taste. Transfer to a serving bowl and garnish with fresh parsley.

Black Beans with Corn and Tomato

Ingredients

- ½ Ib. black beans
- 1 white onion • ½ red onion
- 2 garlic, lightly crushed
- 8 cups water
- 1 cup corn kernels
- 1 tomato, chopped
- ¼ cup minced cilantro
- ½ tsp. ground cumin
- ¼ tsp. smoked paprika
- ¼ tsp. ground black pepper
- ¼ tsp. salt
- 3 tbsp. extra-virgin olive oil
- 3 tbsp. lime juice

Time: 50 min. Servings: 6 Calories: 216

Directions

Add beans, onion, garlic, and water to the Instant Pot. Seal and cook on Bean setting for 30 min. Naturally release pressure for 20 min. Remove onion and garlic, drain, and cool beans. Mix corn, tomato, onion, cilantro, cumin, paprika, pepper, and salt with beans. Whisk oil and juice, pour over bean mixture, and toss. Serve warm.

White Bean and Barley Soup

Ingredients

- 2 tbsp. olive oil
- ½ onion, chopped
- 1 carrot, chopped
- 1 stalk celery, chopped
- 2 garlic, minced
- 2 sprigs fresh thyme
- 1 bay leaf
- ½ tsp. ground black pepper
- 1 can diced tomatoes
- ½ cup pearl barley, drained
- 4 cups vegetable broth
- 2 cups water • ½ tsp. salt
- 2 beans, rinsed

Time: 46 min. Servings: 8 Calories: 126

Directions

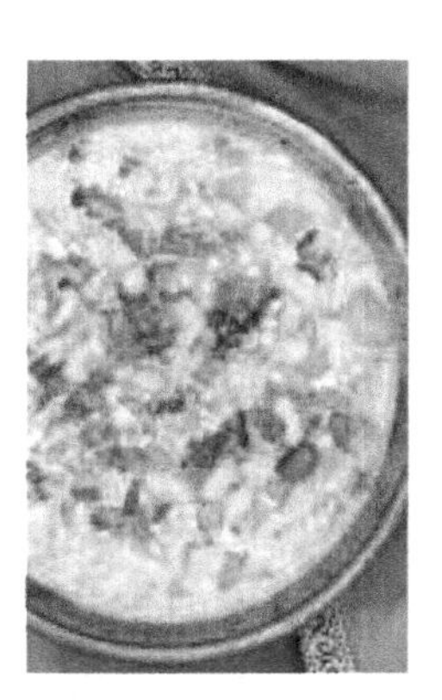

Sauté oil in the Instant Pot. Add onion, carrot, and celery. Cook for 5 min. Add garlic, thyme, bay leaf, and pepper, cook for 30 sec. Press Cancel. Add the tomatoes, barley, broth, and water. Close lid, set to Sealing, press the Soup button, and cook for 20 min. When it beeps, let pressure release naturally, about 20 min. Open lid, stir, add beans and salt. Close lid and Keep Warm for 10 min. Serve.

Greek Green Beans

Ingredients

- ⅓ cup olive oil
- 1 onion (red or white), chopped
- 1 white potato, sliced
- 1 Ib. green beans
- 3 tomatoes, grated
- ¼ cup chopped parsley
- 1 tsp. granulated sugar
- ½ tsp. salt
- ¼ tsp. freshly ground black pepper

Time: 50 min. Servings: 2 Calories: 145

Directions

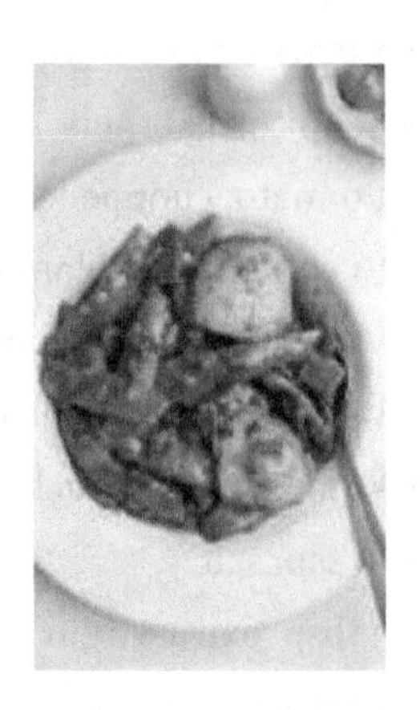

Heat the olive oil in a pot. Add the onions and sauté for 5 min. Add the potatoes, and sauté for 2–3 min. Add green beans and stir. Add tomatoes, parsley, sugar, salt, and black pepper and Stir. Add hot water and simmer for 40 min. Allow the beans to cool until they're warm or until they reach room temperature, but do not serve hot.

Tuscan White Bean Soup

Ingredients

- 30 oz. can cannellini beans, rinsed
- ½ tsp paprika
- 1 tsp dried basil
- ½ tsp red pepper flakes
- 2 cups water
- 4 cups vegetable broth
- 28 oz. tomatoes, diced
- 2 tbsp. olive oil
- 2 bunches Tuscan kale, chopped
- 1 bulb fennel, chopped
- Pepper and Salt, as required

Time: 30 min. Servings: 8 Calories: 172

Directions

Heat olive oil in a large pot over medium-high heat. Add fennel to the pot and sauté for 5 minutes. Add tomatoes and cook for 8 minutes. Add beans, water, and vegetable broth and bring to a boil. Turn heat to low, simmer, and add paprika, basil, red pepper flakes, and salt. Add kale, stir well and cook for 5 minutes. Stir well and serve.

Pasta with Cashew Sauce

Ingredients

- 2 oz. fresh arugula
- ½ cup peas
- 1½ cups broccoli florets
- 1 white onion, diced
- 1 Tbsp. extra-virgin olive oil
- Salt and black pepper, to taste
- 4 sun-dried tomatoes, halved
- 4 oz. whole wheat pasta

Sauce: • ½ cup fresh basil
- ½ cup roasted cashews
- 2 garlic cloves
- 2 Tbsp. lemon juice
- ¼ tsp. sea salt

Time: 25 min. Servings: 2 Calories: 565

Directions

Cook pasta as directed, add broccoli florets before it's done. Reserve 1 cup of pasta water. Blend sauce ingredients until smooth. In a pan, sauté bell peppers, onion, and seasonings. Add tomatoes and arugula, cook for 3 min. Toss in pasta and broccoli, pour sauce, and adjust with pasta water to reach desired consistency. Cook for 4 min, stirring occasionally. Serve warm.

Broccoli and Carrot Pasta Salad

Ingredients

- 8 ounces' whole-wheat pasta
- 2 cups broccoli florets
- 1 cup peeled and shredded carrots
- ¼ cup plain Greek yogurt
- Juice of 1 lemon
- 1 teaspoon red pepper flakes
- Sea salt and freshly ground pepper, to taste

Time: 15 min. Servings: 2 Calories: 428

Directions

Bring a large pot of lightly salted water to a boil. Add the pasta to the boiling water and cook for 8-10 min. Drain the pasta and let rest for a few minutes. When cooled, combine the pasta with the veggies, yogurt, juice, and red pepper flakes in a large bowl, and stir thoroughly to combine. Taste and season to taste with salt and pepper. Serve immediately

Pesto Pasta

Ingredients

Time: 20 min. | Servings: 2 | Calories: 465

- 1 (16 ounce) package spaghetti
- 4 oz. Pecorino-Romano cheese, cut into cubes
- 6 cloves garlic
- 16 oz. loosely packed baby spinach leaves
- 8 oz. firmly packed basil leaves
- 2 oz. chopped walnuts
- 2 oz. lemon juice
- A pinch of lemon zest
- A pinch of salt
- 1 fl oz. olive oil

Directions

Boil 12 oz. of spaghetti for 12 minutes, drain, and transfer to a bowl. In a food processor, blend the Pecorino-Romano until coarsely grated. Add garlic, spinach, basil, walnuts, lemon juice, zest, and salt; process into a thick paste. Drizzle in olive oil while the processor runs, blending until smooth. Pour the pesto sauce over the spaghetti, toss to coat, and serve.

Tomato Basil Pasta

Ingredients

Time: 20 min. | Servings: 2 | Calories: 415

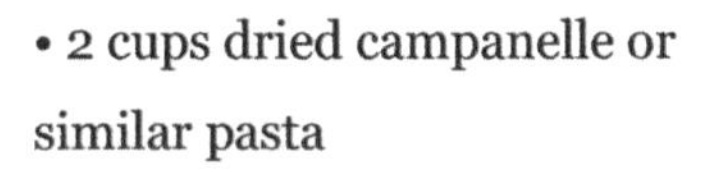

- 2 cups dried campanelle or similar pasta
- 1¾ cups vegetable stock
- ½ tsp. salt
- 2 tomatoes, dices
- 1-2 pinches red pepper flakes
- ½ tsp. garlic powder
- ½ tsp. dried oregano
- 10-12 sweet basil leaves
- Ground black pepper, to taste

Directions

Add pasta, stock, and salt to the Instant Pot, stir. Scatter the tomatoes on top. Secure the lid. Select Manual and cook for 2 min. Once done, do a quick release. Open the lid. Stir in the red pepper, oregano, and garlic powder. Select Sauté and cook for 2 to 3 min. When ready to serve, chiffonade the basil and stir it in. Taste and season with more salt and pepper, as needed. Serve warm.

CHAPTER 3: SIDES, SALADS AND SOUP

Mashed Roasted Eggplant with Spice

Ingredients

- 1 medium eggplant (1 lb.)
- 1 Tbsp. Olive oil
- 2 Tbsp. tahini
- 2 tsp. lemon juice
- 2 garlic cloves, peeled
- 1/8 tsp. salt
- 1/8 tsp. ground nutmeg
- 1/2 tsp. paprika/chili

Time: 50 min. Servings: 4 Calories: 111

Directions

Preheat your oven to 425°F. Wrap garlic cloves and eggplant in foil. Roast garlic for 15 min and eggplant for 40 min. Cool eggplant, peel, and chop. Drain for 5 min. Blend eggplant, roasted garlic, tahini, lemon juice, salt, oil, and nutmeg in a food processor. Transfer to a bowl, garnish with paprika, and serve with wheat bread or vegetable wedges.

Citrus-Marinated Olives

Ingredients

- 2 cups mixed green olives with pits
- 1/4 cup red wine vinegar
- 1/4 cup extra-virgin olive oil
- 4 garlic cloves, finely minced
- Zest and juice of 2 clementine or 1 large orange
- 1 tsp. red pepper flakes
- 2 bay leaves
- 1/2 tsp. ground cumin
- 1/2 tsp. ground allspice

Time: 30 min. Servings: 4 Calories: 147

Directions

In a large glass bowl or jar, combine the olives, vinegar, oil, garlic, orange zest and juice, red pepper flakes, bay leaves, cumin, and allspice and mix well. Cover and refrigerate for at least 4 hours or up to a week to allow the olives to marinate, tossing again before serving.

Olive Tapenade with Anchovies

Ingredients

- 2 cups pitted Kalamata olives
- 2 anchovy fillets, chopped
- 2 tsp. chopped capers
- 1 garlic clove, finely minced
- 1 cooked egg yolk
- 1 tsp. Dijon mustard
- ¼ cup extra-virgin olive oil
- Seedy Crackers
- Versatile Sandwich Round
- Vegetables

Time: 10 min. Servings: 4 Calories: 179

Directions

Rinse the olives in cold water and drain well. In a blender, place the drained olives, anchovies, capers, garlic, egg yolk, and Dijon. Process until thick. With the food processor running, stream in the oil. Transfer to a bowl, and refrigerate at least 1 hr. Serve with Seedy Crackers, atop a Versatile Sandwich Round, or with crunchy vegetables.

Grilled Portobello Mushrooms

Ingredients

- 3 Tbsp. balsamic vinegar
- ½ tsp. onion powder
- 2 Tbsp. avocado oil
- 4 large Portobello mushrooms
- 1 - 2 tsp. liquid smoke
- 1 garlic clove, minced
- Salt, ground pepper
- 3 Tbsp. soy sauce
- 1 Tbsp. Worcestershire sauce

Time: 20 min. Servings: 4 Calories: 49

Directions

Remove the stems from the mushrooms. Combine all ingredients (except the mushrooms and oil) in a bowl and mix. Add the mushrooms to the marinade and let them sit for 20 min. Heat a grill or pan to medium-high heat. Brush the surface with oil and arrange the mushrooms in one layer. Cook for 5 min. on each side. Serve as appetizer or in a sandwich

Pasta Salad with Pine Nuts

Ingredients

- 4 cups whole wheat penne pasta
- 1/4 cup toasted pine nuts
- 4 tbsps. olive oil
- Pinch of sea salt
- 1 bunch chopped fresh basil
- 2 cups halved tomatoes
- 1/8 tsp. cracked black pepper
- 1 cup chopped mozzarella cheese

Time: 35 min. Servings: 4 Calories: 388

Directions

Boil water in a large pot and. Add little oil. Add the pasta, stir once and cook for 8-10 min. Remove and set aside. In a pan, heat the pine nuts, stirring constantly to prevent from burning. Bake for about 2 min. until the nuts light brown. Add the warm pasta and the remaining ingredients in a bowl and stir. Divide into 4 portions and serve warm.

Taverna-Style Greek Salad

Ingredients

- 4-5 tomatoes, chopped
- 1 cucumber, chopped
- 1 green bell pepper, sliced
- 1 small red onion, sliced
- 16 pitted Kalamata olives
- 1/4 cup capers, or more olives
- 1 tsp. dried oregano, divided
- 1/2 cup extra-virgin olive oil, divided
- 1 pack feta cheese
- Optional: salt, pepper, and fresh oregano, for garnish

Time: 20 min. Servings: 4 Calories: 320

Directions

Place the vegetables in a large serving bowl. Add the olives, capers, feta, half of the dried oregano and half of the olive oil. Mix to combine. Place the whole piece of feta cheese on top, sprinkle with the remaining dried oregano, and drizzle with the remaining olive oil. Season to taste and serve immediately.

Baked Arugula and Acorn Squash Salad

Ingredients

- Extra-virgin olive oil, for coating squash
- 4 cups arugula
- 1 medium acorn squash, cut into rounds
- ½ cup Brussels sprouts, shaved or thinly sliced
- ⅓ cup pomegranate seeds
- ¼ cup pumpkin seeds

Time: 30 min. Servings: 3 Calories: 113

Directions

Preheat the oven to 400°F. Line a baking sheet with parchment paper. Arrange the squash on the baking sheet and toss with oil to coat well. Place in a layer and bake for 20 min. Combine the arugula, Brussels sprouts, pomegranate, and pumpkin seeds in a bowl, and toss with the dressing. Place the squash on top and drizzle with dressing on top. Enjoy!

Green Mediterranean Salad

Ingredients

- 1 head lettuce, chopped
- 2 cucumbers, peeled and sliced
- 3 spring onions (white parts only), sliced
- ½ cup chopped fresh dill
- ⅓ cup extra virgin olive oil
- 2 tbsp. fresh lemon juice
- ¼ tsp. fine sea salt
- 4 ounces crumbled feta
- 7 Kalamata olives, pitted

Time: 15 min. Servings: 4 Calories: 284

Directions

Add lettuce, cucumber, spring onions, and dill to a bowl. Toss to combine. In a bowl, whisk the oil and lemon juice. Pour the dressing over the salad, toss, then sprinkle the salt over the top. Sprinkle the feta and olives over the top and then gently toss the salad one more time. Serve promptly.

Greek Salad with Lemon Vinaigrette

Ingredients

- ½ red onion, thinly sliced
- ¼ cup extra-virgin olive oil
- 3 tbsp. fresh lemon juice
- 1 clove garlic, minced
- ½ tsp. dried oregano
- ½ tsp. ground black pepper
- ¼ tsp. kosher salt
- 4 tomatoes
- 1 cucumber, diced
- 1 yellow or red bell pepper
- ½ cup Kalamata olives
- ¼ cup chopped parsley
- 4 ounces feta cheese, cubes

Time: 30 min. Servings: 8 Calories: 190

Directions

In a bowl, soak the onion in water to for 10 min. In a bowl, combine the oil, lemon juice or vinegar, garlic, oregano, black pepper, and salt. Drain and add to a large bowl with the tomatoes, cucumber, bell pepper, olives, and parsley. Toss the vegetables. Pour the vinaigrette over the salad. Add the cheese and toss again to distribute. Serve, or chill for 30 min.

Powerhouse Arugula Salad

Ingredients

- 4 tbsp. extra-virgin olive oil
- Zest and juice of
- 1 orange (2 to 3 tablespoons)
- 1 tbsp. red wine vinegar
- ½ teaspoon salt
- ¼ tsp. ground black pepper
- 8 cups baby arugula
- 1 cup chopped walnuts
- 1 cup crumbled feta cheese
- ½ cup pomegranate seeds

Time: 10 min. Servings: 4 Calories: 448

Directions

In a small bowl, whisk together the olive oil, zest and juice, vinegar, salt, and pepper and set aside.

To assemble the salad for serving, in a large bowl, combine the arugula, walnuts, goat cheese, and pomegranate seeds. Drizzle with the dressing and toss to coat.

White Bean Soup with Kale and Lemon

Ingredients

- 1 tbsp. light olive oil
- 2 stalks celery, chopped
- 1 yellow onion, chopped
- 2 cloves garlic, minced
- 1 tbsp. chopped oregano
- 4 cups chopped kale
- 1 Ib. dried beans, soaked overnight
- 8 cups vegetable broth
- ¼ cup lemon juice
- 1 tbsp. extra-virgin olive oil
- 1 tsp. ground black pepper

Time: 42 min. Servings: 8 Calories: 129

Directions

Press Sauté on the Instant Pot and heat olive oil. Cook celery and onion for 5 min, then add garlic and oregano for 30 sec. Stir in kale and cook for 1 min. Press Cancel, then add beans, broth, lemon juice, olive oil, and pepper. Close the lid, set to Sealing, and cook on Manual for 20 min. Allow natural pressure release for 20 min. Open the lid, stir, and serve hot.

Creamy Yellow Lentil Soup

Ingredients

- 2 tablespoons olive oil
- 1 medium yellow onion, peeled and chopped
- 1 medium carrot, peeled and chopped
- 2 garlic, peeled and minced
- 1 teaspoon ground cumin
- ½ tsp. ground black pepper
- ¼ tsp. salt
- 2 cups dried yellow lentils, rinsed and drained
- 6 cups water

Time: 10 min. Servings: 4 Calories: 448

Directions

Sauté the oil in the Instant Pot. Add onion and carrot and cook for 3 min. Add garlic, cumin, pepper, and salt and cook for 30 sec. Press the Cancel. Add lentils and water, close lid, set steam release to Sealing, press Manual, and set time to 15 min. When it beeps, let pressure release naturally, about 15 min. Open lid and purée with a blender in batches. Serve warm.

Chicken Gnocchi Soup

Ingredients

- 2 tbsp. olive oil
- 1 onion, diced
- 2 garlic cloves, minced
- 2 carrots, diced
- 2 celery stalks, diced
- 1 Ib. chicken breast, pieces
- 4 cup chicken broth
- 1 tsp. dried basil
- 1 tsp. dried oregano
- Salt and pepper to taste
- 1 cup whole wheat gnocchi
- 2 cups spinach, chopped
- ¼ cup Parmesan cheese

Time: 45 min. Servings: 4 Calories: 350

Directions

Heat oil in a pot over heat. Sauté onion and garlic until translucent. Add carrots and celery, cook for 5 min. Increase heat, add chicken, and cook until no longer pink. Pour in chicken broth, water, and seasonings. Bring to a boil, then simmer and add gnocchi. Cook until tender. Stir in spinach and cook until wilted. Serve hot, optionally garnished with Parmesan

Ginger Chicken with Vegetable Soup

Ingredients

- 3 cups shredded rotisserie chicken, skin removed
- 8 cups no-salt-added chicken broth
- 2 tbsps. extra-virgin olive oil
- 1 tbsp. grated fresh ginger
- 1 onion, chopped
- 2 red bell peppers, chopped
- ½ tsp. sea salt
- ⅛ tsp. freshly ground black pepper

Time: 20 min. Servings: 4 Calories: 348

Directions

Heat the olive oil in a large pot over medium-high heat, until it shimmers. Stir in the ginger, onion and red bell peppers. Cook until the vegetables are soft, about 5 minutes, stirring occasionally. Add the chicken, chicken broth, pepper and salt, stir well and bring to a simmer. Reduce the heat to medium-low and simmer for 5 minutes.

CHAPTER 4: SANDWICHES, PIZZAS AND WRAPS

Tuna Salad Sandwich

Ingredients

- 1 can tuna, drained
- ¼ cup Greek yogurt
- 1 tbsp. lemon juice
- ¼ cup diced cucumber
- ¼ cup halved cherry tomatoes
- 2 tbsp. diced red onion
- 2 tbsp. sliced olives
- 1 tbsp. chopped parsley
- Salt and black pepper, to taste
- 4 slices whole-grain bread
- 1 cup shredded lettuce
- ½ lbs. ripe avocado, sliced

Time: 10 min. | Servings: 2 | Calories: 320

Directions

Heat oil over medium heat, sauté onion and garlic until translucent. Add carrots, celery, and cook for 5 min. Add chicken, cook until no longer pink. Pour in broth, water, herbs, and bring to a boil. Simmer with gnocchi until tender. Stir in spinach, cook until wilted. Serve hot with Parmesan.

Greek Salad Wraps

Ingredients

- 1½ cups cucumber, chopped
- 1 cup chopped tomato
- ½ cup finely chopped mint
- 1 can sliced black olives
- ¼ cup diced red onion
- 2 tbsp. extra-virgin olive oil
- 1 tbsp. red wine vinegar
- ¼ tsp. ground black pepper
- ¼ tsp. kosher or sea salt
- ½ cup crumbled goat cheese
- 4 whole-wheat flatbread wraps

Time: 15 min. | Servings: 4 | Calories: 217

Directions

In a bowl, mix cucumber, tomato, mint, olives, and onion until combined. In a small bowl, mix oil, vinegar, pepper, and salt. Drizzle over the salad, and mix. Spread the cheese evenly over the four wraps. Spoon a quarter of the salad down the middle of each wrap. Fold, repeat and serve.

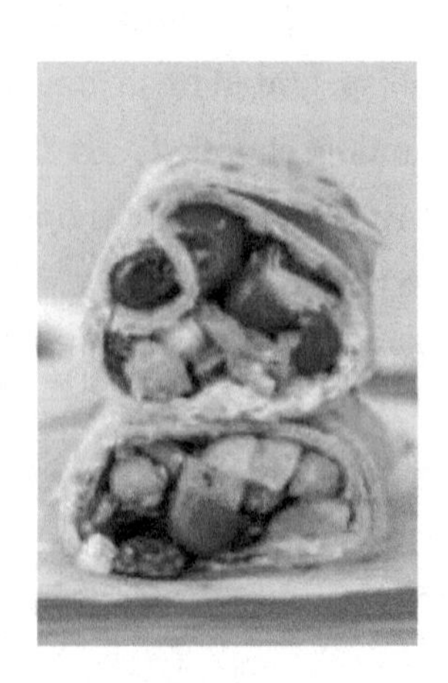

Margherita Open-Face Sandwiches

Ingredients

- 2 whole-wheat bread, sliced
- 1 tbsp. olive oil
- 1 garlic clove, halved
- 1 large ripe tomato, cut into 8 slices
- ¼ teaspoon dried oregano
- 1 cup fresh mozzarella, sliced
- ¼ cup basil, torn into small pieces
- ¼ tsp. freshly ground black pepper

Time: 15 min. Servings: 4 Calories: 176

Directions

Preheat the broiler with the rack 4 inches below the heating element. Place bread on a baking sheet and broil for 1 min. Remove from the oven, brush with oil, and rub each piece with a garlic half. Add tomato and sprinkle with oregano. Layer cheese on top. Return the sheet to the broiler and cook for 1½ min. Once done, top with fresh basil and pepper.

Grilled Eggplant and Feta Sandwiches

Ingredients

- 1 medium eggplant, sliced into ½-inch-thick slices
- 2 tbsp. olive oil
- Sea salt and freshly ground pepper, to taste
- 5 to 6 tbsp. hummus
- 4 slices whole-wheat bread, toasted
- 1 cup baby spinach leaves
- 2 ounces feta cheese, softened

Time: 18 min. Servings: 2 Calories: 516

Directions

Preheat a grill to medium-high heat. Salt both sides of the eggplant, and let sit for 20 min. Rinse the eggplant and pat dry with a paper towel. Brush the eggplant with oil and season with salt and pepper. Grill until for 4 min on both side. Spread the hummus on the bread and top with the spinach, feta, and eggplant. Top with the other bread slice and serve warm.

Cucumber Hummus Sandwiches

Ingredients

- 1 large cucumber, thinly sliced
- 8 slices whole grain bread
- 1 cup hummus
- 1 small red onion, thinly sliced
- 1 medium tomato, sliced
- 2 tbsp. fresh parsley, chopped
- Salt and pepper to taste

Time: 10 min. Servings: 4 Calories: 250

Directions

Lay the slices of bread on a clean surface. Spread hummus on one side of each bread slice. Arrange the cucumber over 4 slices of bread. Top the cucumber with onion and tomato. Sprinkle parsley over the vegetables. Season with salt and pepper to taste. Place the remaining slices of bread on top to form sandwiches. Cut each sandwich in half to serve.

Vegetable Pita Sandwiches

Ingredients

- 1 baby eggplant, peeled and chopped
- 1 red bell pepper, sliced
- ½ cup diced red onion
- ½ cup shredded carrot
- 1 tsp. olive oil
- ⅓ cup low-fat Greek yogurt
- ½ tsp. dried tarragon
- 2 low-sodium whole-wheat pita breads, halved crosswise

Time: 20 min. Servings: 4 Calories: 115

Directions

In a baking pan, stir the eggplant, red bell pepper, onion, carrot, and oil. Put the mix into the air fryer and roast at 390°F for 7-9 min. Drain. In a bowl, mix the yogurt and tarragon until combined. Stir the yogurt mix into the vegetables. Stuff ¼ of this mix into each pita pocket. Place the sandwiches in the air fryer and cook for 3 min. Serve immediately.

Flatbread Pizza with Tomatoes, and Feta

Ingredients

- 1½ Ib. cherry or grape tomatoes, halved
- 3 tbsp. olive oil, divided
- ½ teaspoon salt
- ½ tsp. ground black pepper
- 4 flatbread rounds
- 1 can artichoke hearts, rinsed, and cut into thin wedges
- 8 oz. crumbled feta cheese
- ¼ cup chopped fresh Greek oregano

Time: 25 min. 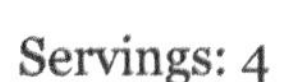 Servings: 4 Calories: 436

Directions

Preheat the oven to 500°F. Toss tomatoes with 1 tbsp. olive oil, salt, and pepper, then spread on a baking sheet. Roast for 10-12 min. Remove and reduce oven to 450°F. Place breads on a baking sheet, brush with 2 tbsp. oil, and top with artichoke hearts, tomatoes, and cheese, divided equally. Bake for 8-10 min. Sprinkle oregano on top and serve.

Beef and Bean Pizza

Ingredients

- ¾ cup refried beans (from a 16-ounce can)
- ½ cup salsa
- 10 frozen precooked beef meatballs, thawed and sliced
- 1 jalapeño pepper, sliced
- 4 whole-wheat pita breads
- 1 cup shredded pepper Jack cheese
- ½ cup shredded Colby cheese
- ⅓ cup sour cream

Time: 20 min. Servings: 4 Calories: 484

Directions

In a medium bowl, combine the refried beans, salsa, meatballs, and jalapeño pepper. Preheat the air fryer for 3-4 minutes or until hot. Top the pitas with the refried bean mixture and sprinkle with the cheeses. Bake at 370°F for 7-9 min. Top each pizza with a dollop of sour cream and serve warm.

Classic Margherita Pizza

Ingredients

Time: 20 min. Servings: 4 Calories: 570

- All-purpose flour, for dusting
- 1-pound premade pizza dough
- 1 can crushed tomatoes, with their juices
- 2 garlic cloves
- 1 tsp. Italian seasoning
- Pinch sea salt, plus more as needed
- 1½ tsp. olive oil
- 10 slices mozzarella cheese
- 12 t15 fresh basil leaves

Directions

Preheat the oven to 475°F. Roll the dough into a 12-inch round on a floured surface and place on a baking sheet. In a food processor, blend tomatoes with juices, garlic, Italian seasoning, and salt until smooth. Adjust seasoning to taste. Drizzle oil over the dough, spread the sauce, and add mozzarella. Bake for 8-10 min. Let sit for 1-2 min after baking. Top with basil before serving.

Pesto Chicken Mini Pizzas

Ingredients

Time: 15 min. Servings: 4 Calories: 617

- • 2 cups shredded cooked chicken
- ¾ cup pesto
- 4 English muffins, split
- 2 cups shredded Mozzarella cheese

Directions

In a medium bowl, toss the chicken with the pesto. Place one-eighth of the chicken on each English muffin half. Top each English muffin with ¼ cup of the Mozzarella cheese. Put four pizzas at a time in the air fryer and air fry at 350°F for 5 minutes. Repeat this process with the other four pizzas.

Avocado and Asparagus Wraps

Ingredients

Time: 20 min. Servings: 6 Calories: 361

- 12 spears asparagus
- 1 ripe avocado, mashed
- Juice of 1 lime
- 2 cloves garlic, minced
- 2 cups brown rice, cooked
- 3 tablespoons Greek yogurt
- Sea salt and ground pepper, to taste
- 3 (8-inch) whole-grain tortillas
- ½ cup cilantro, diced
- 2 tbsp. red onion, diced

Directions

Steam asparagus in a stove-top steamer until tender. Mash avocado, lime juice, and garlic in a bowl. In another bowl, mix rice and yogurt. Season both mix with salt and pepper to taste. Heat tortillas in a skillet. Spread each tortilla with avocado mixture, top with rice, cilantro, onion, and asparagus. Fold sides and roll tightly. Cut diagonally before serving.

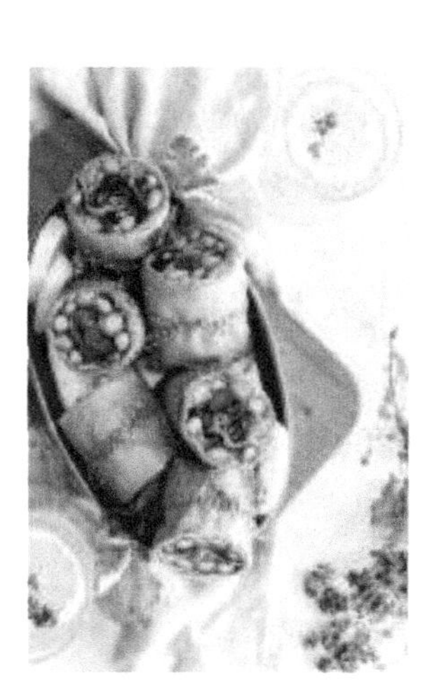

Falafel Wraps

Ingredients

Time: 20 min. Servings: 4 Calories: 350

1 cup canned chickpeas, rinsed
1/4 cup chopped onion
2 cloves garlic, minced
1 tsp. ground cumin
1 tsp. ground coriander
1/2 tsp. baking powder
2 tbsp. all-purpose flour
Salt and pepper to taste
2 tbsp. olive oil
4 whole wheat wraps
1 cup mixed greens
1/2 cup tomatoes, halved
1/2 cup cucumber, sliced
1/4 cup tahini sauce

Directions

In a food processor, combine the chickpeas, onion, garlic, 1/4 cup parsley, cumin, coriander, baking powder, flour, salt, and pepper. Pulse until the mix is finely ground. Form the mix into small patties. Heat the oil in a skillet over medium heat. Fry the patties for 3-4 min per side. Warm the wraps in and fill with mixed greens, tomatoes, cucumber, and patties. Drizzle with tahini sauce.

Jerk Chicken Wraps

Ingredients

- 1 Ib. boneless, skinless chicken tenderloins
- 1 cup jerk marinade Olive oil
- 4 large low-carb tortillas
- 1 cup julienned carrots
- 1 cup peeled cucumber ribbons
- 1 cup shredded lettuce
- 1 cup mango or pineapple chunks

Time: 45 min. Servings: 4 Calories: 241

Directions

Coat chicken with jerk marinade, cover, and refrigerate. Spray air fryer basket with oil and add chicken. Air fry at 375°F for 8 min, turning chicken and brushing with marinade. Cook until 165°F, 5-7 min. Fill each tortilla with 1/4 cup carrot, cucumber, lettuce, and mango, then top with 1/4 chicken tenderloins. Roll up and serve warm or cold.

Roasted Red Pepper and Hummus Wrap

Ingredients

- 4 whole wheat wraps
- 1 cup hummus
- 2 roasted red peppers, sliced
- 1 cup spinach leaves
- 1/2 cup shredded carrots
- 1/4 cup crumbled feta cheese
- 2 tablespoons olive oil
- Salt and pepper to taste

Time: 10 min. Servings: 2 Calories: 300

Directions

Spread a generous amount of hummus on each whole wheat wrap. Layer with sliced roasted red peppers, spinach leaves, shredded carrots, and crumbled feta cheese. Drizzle with oil and season with salt and pepper. Roll up each wrap tightly and cut in half if desired. Serve immediately as a light lunch.

CHAPTER 5: VEGETABLE MAIN

Crispy Eggplant Rounds

Ingredients

- 1 eggplant, cut into ½-inch slice
- ½ teaspoon salt
- 2 ounces Parmesan cheese crisps, finely ground
- ½ teaspoon paprika
- ¼ teaspoon garlic powder
- 1 large egg

Time: 20 min. Servings: 4 Calories: 113

Directions

Rinse and dry kale, then tear into bite-sized pieces. Heat 1 tbsp. olive oil in a large skillet, add garlic, and cook for 1 min. Add kale and cook until wilted. Add tomatoes and cook until softened. Remove from heat, season with sea salt and ground pepper, drizzle with remaining olive oil and lemon juice, then serve. Enjoy!

Crustless Spinach Cheese Pie

Ingredients

- 6 large eggs
- ¼ cup heavy cream
- 1 cup frozen chopped spinach
- 1 cup shredded sharp
- Cheddar cheese
- ¼ cup diced yellow onion

Time: 30 min. Servings: 4 Calories: 263

Directions

In a medium bowl, whisk eggs and add cream. Add remaining ingredients to bowl. Pour into a round baking dish. Place into the air fryer basket. Adjust the temperature to 320°F and bake for 20 min. Eggs will be firm and slightly browned when cooked. Serve immediately.

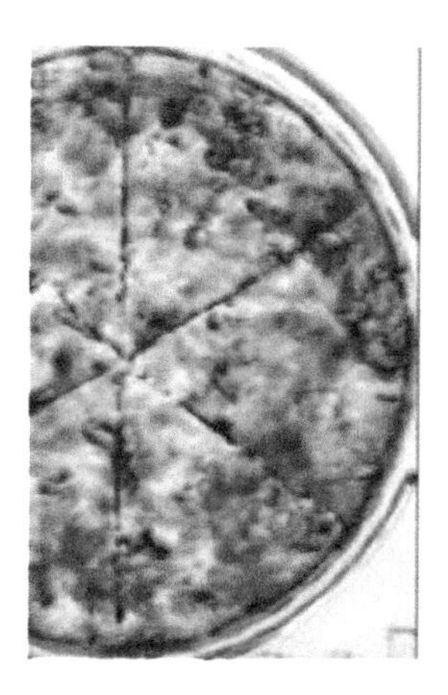

Steamed Asparagus

Ingredients

- 7 asparagus spears, trimmed
- ¼ tsp. pepper
- 1 tbsp. extra virgin olive oil
- Juice from freshly squeezed ¼ lemon
- ¼ tsp. salt
- 1 cup water

Time: 10 min. Servings: 1 Calories: 108

Directions

Place the steamer rack in the Instant Pot and pour in the water. In a mixing bowl, combine the asparagus spears, salt, pepper, and lemon juice. Place on top of the trivet. Lock the lid. Set the Instant Pot to Steam mode, then set the timer for 5 min. at High Pressure. Once complete, do a quick release. Carefully open the lid. Drizzle the asparagus with olive oil.

Simple Oven-baked Green Beans

Ingredients

- 2 tbsp. olive oil
- 2 lb. green beans, trimmed
- Salt and black pepper to taste

Time: 15 min. Servings: 6 Calories: 157

Directions

Preheat the oven to 400°F. Toss the beans with olive oil and salt, then spread them in a single layer on a greased baking dish. Roast for 8-10 min. Transfer to a serving platter and drizzle with the remaining olive oil before serving.

Parmesan Stuffed Zucchini Boats

Ingredients

- 1 cup chickpeas, rinsed
- 1 cup no-sugar-added spaghetti sauce
- 2 zucchinis
- ¼ cup shredded Parmesan cheese

Time: 15 min. Servings: 4 Calories: 139

Directions

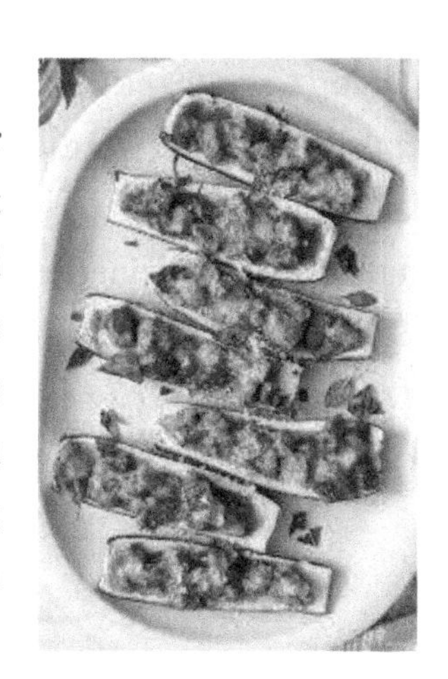

Preheat the oven to 425°F. In a bowl, stir the chickpeas and spaghetti sauce. Cut the zucchini in half lengthwise and scrape down the length to remove the seeds. Fill each zucchini with the chickpea sauce and top with ¼ Parmesan cheese. Place the halves on a baking sheet and roast for 15 min. Transfer to a plate. Let rest for 5 min. before serving.

Simple Sautéed Cauliflower

Ingredients

- Salt and freshly ground black pepper, to taste
- 1 medium head cauliflower, cut into florets
- 2 tablespoons olive oil
- 2 garlic cloves, minced
- A pinch of red pepper flakes

Time: 15 min. Servings: 2 Calories: 116

Directions

Heat the olive oil in a large skillet over medium heat. Add the cauliflower florets to the skillet. If using garlic or red pepper flakes, add them now. Sauté the cauliflower for about 8-10 min, stirring occasionally, until the florets are golden brown and tender. Season with salt and freshly ground black pepper. Serve immediately.

Kale and Beet Grain Bowl

Ingredients

Time: 10 min. | Servings: 2 | Calories: 350

- 1 cup precooked quinoa
- 2 cups kale, chopped
- 1 cup precooked beets, diced
- ¼ cup walnuts, chopped
- 2 tbsp. feta cheese, crumbled
- 2 tbsp. olive oil
- 1 tbsp. balsamic vinegar
- Salt and pepper to taste
- Optional: ¼ cup pomegranate seeds

Directions

In a bowl, mix the quinoa, chopped kale, and diced beets. Whisk olive oil, balsamic vinegar, salt, and pepper in a small bowl. Pour the dressing over the quinoa mixture and toss until everything is well coated. Divide the mixture into two serving bowls. Top each bowl with walnuts, feta cheese, and optional pomegranate seeds. Serve immediately

Greek Stewed Zucchini

Ingredients

Time: 45 min. | Servings: 4-6 | Calories: 183

- ¼ cup extra-virgin olive oil
- 1 small yellow onion, slivered
- 4 zucchini squash, cut into ½-inch-thick rounds
- 4 garlic cloves, minced
- 1-2 tsp. dried oregano
- 2 cups chopped tomatoes
- ½ cup halved and pitted Kalamata olives
- ¾ cup crumbled feta cheese
- ¼ cup chopped parsley

Directions

In a large skillet, heat the oil over medium-high heat. Add the onion and sauté until just tender. Add the zucchini, garlic, and oregano and sauté another 6-8 min. Add the tomatoes and bring to a boil. Reduce the heat and add the olives. Cover and simmer for 20 min. Serve warm topped with feta and parsley.

Spinach-Artichoke Stuffed Mushrooms

Ingredients

- 2 tbsp. olive oil
- 4 Portobello mushrooms
- ½ tsp. salt
- ¼ tsp. ground pepper
- 4 oz. feta cheese, crumbled
- ½ cup chopped marinated artichoke hearts
- 1 cup frozen spinach, thawed
- ½ cup grated Parmesan cheese
- 2 tbsp. chopped fresh parsley

Time: 24 min. | Servings: 4 | Calories: 287

Directions

Preheat the air fryer to 400°F. Rub olive oil over Portobello mushrooms, coating them. Sprinkle with salt and black pepper, then place top-side down. Mix feta cheese, artichoke, and spinach in a bowl until combined. Divide among mushrooms, sprinkle with Parmesan cheese, and air fry for 10-14 min. Top with fresh parsley before serving.

Sweet and Crispy Roasted Pearl Onions

Ingredients

- 1 (14½ oz.) package frozen pearl onions
- 2 tbsp. extra-virgin olive oil
- 2 tbsp. balsamic vinegar
- 2 tsp. finely chopped fresh rosemary
- ½ tsp. kosher salt
- ¼ tsp. black pepper

Time: 23 min. | Servings: 3 | Calories: 118

Directions

In a medium bowl, combine the onions, olive oil, vinegar, rosemary, salt, and pepper until well coated.

Transfer the onions to the air fryer basket. Set the air fryer to 400°F for 18 min, stirring once or twice during the cooking time.

Chickpea Sauce with Fusilli

Ingredients

Time: 35 min. | Servings: 4 | Calories: 310

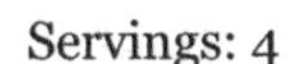

- ¼ cup extra-virgin olive oil
- ½ large shallot, chopped
- 5 garlic cloves, thinly sliced
- 15-oz. chickpeas, drained
- ½ cup canning liquid
- Pinch red pepper flakes
- 1 cup whole-grain fusilli pasta
- ¼ tsp. salt
- ⅛ tsp. ground black pepper
- ¼ cup Parmesan cheese
- ¼ cup chopped fresh basil
- 2 tsp. dried parsley
- 1 tsp. dried oregano

Directions

In a pan, heat oil and sauté shallot and garlic for 3–5 min. Add ¾ chickpeas with 2 tbsp. liquid and simmer. Blend until smooth, then mix in remaining chickpeas. Cook pasta in salted water for 8 min. Reserve ½ cup pasta water, drain, and return pasta to pot. Add sauce and pasta water, and heat. Season with salt and pepper. Serve with cheese, basil, parsley, oregano, and pepper flakes.

Pistachio Mint Pesto Pasta

Ingredients

Time: 20 min. | Servings: 4 | Calories: 420

- 8 oz. whole-wheat pasta
- 1 cup fresh mint
- ½ cup fresh basil
- ⅓ cup unsalted pistachios, shelled
- 1 garlic clove, peeled
- ½ tsp. kosher salt
- Juice of ½ lime
- ⅓ cup extra-virgin olive oil

Directions

Cook the pasta according to the package directions. Drain, leaving ½ cup of the water, and set aside. In a food processor, add the mint, basil, pistachios, garlic, salt, and lime juice. Process until the pistachios are coarsely ground. Add the olive oil and process until incorporated. In a large bowl, mix the pasta with the pistachio pesto to incorporate.

Sicilian Caponata

Ingredients

- 3 eggplants, dice
- 1 red onion, peeled and diced
- 1 small branch rosemary
- 2 stems of celery, diced
- 1 carrot, diced
- ½ cup olive oil
- 4 cloves of garlic, sliced
- 6 ripe, tomatoes, diced
- 2 tbsp. capers, drained
- 1 tbsp. sultanas or raisins
- ⅓ cup red wine vinegar
- Salt and pepper
- 4 slices of wholegrain bread

Time: 45 min. Servings: 4 Calories: 510

Directions

Warm olive oil in a large skillet over heat. Fry the eggplant for 5-6 min, then lift out with a spoon. Add onion, carrot, and celery with a pinch of salt. Fry for about 10 min., then add garlic, tomatoes, capers, and raisins. Once tomatoes start collapsing, add vinegar and return eggplant. Boil, reduce heat, and simmer for 20 min. Adjust seasoning, turn off heat, and cool. Serve with bread.

Quinoa and Chickpea Stuffed Peppers

Ingredients

- 4 bell peppers, halved and seeds removed
- 1 cup cooked quinoa
- 1 can chickpeas, drained
- 1 cup tomatoes, halved
- ½ cup crumbled feta cheese
- ¼ cup parsley, chopped
- 2 tbsp. red wine vinegar
- 3 tbsp. olive oil
- Salt and pepper to taste

Time: 30 min. Servings: 4 Calories: 220

Directions

Turn the oven on to 375°F, or 190°C. Combine the quinoa, chickpeas, tomatoes, feta, parsley, olive oil, red wine vinegar, and salt and pepper in a bowl. Place a filling of the quinoa mixture inside each pepper half. Bake peppers for 30 min., or until soft. Top with a last pinch of feta before serving.

CHAPTER 6: FISH & SEAFOOD

Garlic Parmesan Shrimp

Ingredients

- 1 Ib. shrimp, peeled
- ½ cup parmesan cheese, grated
- ¼ cup cilantro, diced
- 1 tbsp. olive oil
- 1 tsp. salt
- 1 tsp. fresh cracked pepper
- 1 tbsp. lemon juice
- 6 garlic cloves, diced

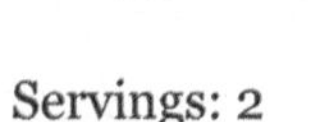

Time: 30 min. Servings: 2 Calories: 602

Directions

Preheat the Air fryer to 350°F and grease an Air fryer basket. Drizzle shrimp with olive oil and lemon juice and season with garlic, salt and cracked pepper. Cover the bowl with plastic wrap and refrigerate for about 3 hours. Stir in the parmesan cheese and cilantro to the bowl and transfer to the Air fryer basket. Air fry for about 10 min. and serve immediately.

Crispy Salmon Fillets

Ingredients

- 1 tbsp. avocado oil
- 2 (3 oz.) salmon fillets
- 1 tsp. paprika
- ½ tsp. salt
- ¼ tsp. dried thyme
- ¼ tsp. onion powder
- ¼ tsp. pepper
- ⅛ tsp. cayenne pepper

Time: 10 min. Servings: 2 Calories: 205

Directions

Drizzle the avocado oil over salmon fillets. Combine the remaining ingredients in a small bowl and rub all over fillets. Press the Sauté button on the Instant Pot. Add the salmon fillets and sear for 2 to 5 min. until the salmon easily flakes with a fork. Serve warm.

Tomato Tuna Melts

Ingredients

Time: 10 min. Servings: 2 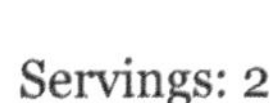 Calories: 244

- 5 oz. tuna, drained
- 2 tbsp. plain Greek yogurt
- 2 tbsp. chopped celery
- 1 tbsp. finely chopped red onion
- 2 tbsp. squeezed lemon juice
- Pinch cayenne pepper
- 1 large tomato, cut into ¾-inch-thick rounds
- ½ cup shredded Cheddar cheese

Directions

Preheat the broiler to High. Stir together the tuna, yogurt, celery, red onion, lemon juice, and cayenne pepper in a medium bowl. Place the tomato rounds on a baking sheet. Top each with some tuna salad and Cheddar cheese. Broil for 3 to 4 min. until the cheese is melted and bubbly. Cool for 5 min. before serving.

Spicy Sardines Fillets

Ingredients

Time: 10 min. Servings: 4 Calories: 794

- Avocado oil, as needed
- 1½ Ib. whole fresh sardines, scales removed
- 1 tsp. salt
- 1 tsp. freshly ground black pepper
- 2 cups flour

Directions

Season the fish with the salt and pepper. Dredge the fish in the flour so it is completely covered. Slowly drop in 1 fish at a time, making sure not to overcrowd the pan. Cook for about 3 min. on each side. Serve warm..

Breaded Shrimp

Ingredients

Time: 15 min. Servings: 4 Calories: 714

- 2 large eggs
- 1 tbsp. water
- 2 cups seasoned Italian bread crumbs
- 1 tsp. salt
- 1 cup flour
- 1 Ib. large shrimp (21 to 25), peeled and deveined
- Extra-virgin olive oil, as needed

Directions

In a small bowl, beat the eggs with water, then transfer to a shallow dish. Mix bread crumbs and salt in another shallow dish, and place flour in a third dish. Coat shrimp in flour, then egg, and finally bread crumbs. Heat a skillet over high heat with olive oil. Cook shrimp for 2–3 min. per side. Drain on paper towels and serve warm.

Maple Glazed Salmon

Ingredients

Time: 18 min. Servings: 2 Calories: 277

- 2 (6-ounces) salmon fillets
- Salt, to taste
- 2 tbsps. maple syrup

Directions

Preheat the Air fryer to 355°F and grease an Air fryer basket. Coat the salmon fillets evenly with maple syrup and season with salt. Arrange the salmon fillets into the Air fryer basket and air fry for about 8 minutes. Remove from the Air fryer and dish out the salmon fillets to serve hot.

Fettuccine with Spinach and Shrimp

Ingredients

Time: 20 min. Servings: 4-6 Calories: 418

- 8 oz. whole-wheat fettuccine pasta, uncooked
- 3 garlic cloves, peeled, chopped
- 2 tsp. dried basil, crushed
- 12 oz. shrimp, peeled
- ¼ tsp. red pepper flakes
- ½ cup crumbled feta cheese
- 1 teaspoon salt
- 10 oz. frozen spinach, thawed
- 1 cup sour cream

Directions

In a large bowl, combine sour cream, feta, basil, garlic, salt, and red pepper. According to the package instructions, cook the fettucine. After the first 8 min. of cooking, add spinach and shrimp to the boiling water with pasta; boil for 2 min. more and drain thoroughly. Add the hot pasta, spinach, and shrimp mixture into the bowl with the sour cream mix; lightly toss and serve immediately.

Healthy Tuna & Bean Wraps

Ingredients

Time: 10 min. Servings: 4 Calories: 279

- 15 oz. canned cannellini beans
- 12 oz. canned light tuna
- 1/8 tsp. white pepper
- 1/8 tsp. kosher salt
- 1 tbsp. fresh parsley, chopped
- 2 tbsp. extra-virgin oil
- ¼ cup red onion, chopped
- 12 romaine lettuce leaves
- 1 medium-sized ripe
- Hass avocado, sliced

Directions

In a bowl, stir the beans, tuna, pepper, salt, parsley, avocado oil, and red onions. Spoon some of the mixture onto each lettuce leaf. Top with the sliced avocado before folding and serving.

Citrus-Glazed Salmon with Zucchini Noodles

Ingredients

- 4 (5-6-oz.) pieces salmon
- ½ tsp. kosher salt
- ¼ tsp. ground black pepper
- 1 tbsp. extra-virgin olive oil
- 1 cup squeezed orange juice
- 1 tsp. low-sodium soy sauce
- 2 zucchinis, spiralized
- 1 tbsp. fresh chives, chopped
- 1 tbsp. fresh parsley, chopped

Time: 30 min. | Servings: 4 | Calories: 280

Directions

Preheat the oven to 350°F. Season the salmon with salt and pepper. Heat olive oil in a pan over high. Sear the salmon, skin side down, for 5 min. Flip and transfer to the oven for 5-9 min. Set aside. In the same pan, deglaze with juice and sauce, simmer and scrap bits for 5-7 min. Serve salmon on zucchini noodles, drizzled with orange glaze, and garnish with chives and parsley.

Garlicky Broiled Sardines

Ingredients

- 16 sardines, packed in water
- 2 tbsp. extra-virgin olive oil
- 4 garlic cloves, minced
- ½ tsp. red pepper flakes
- ½ teaspoon salt
- ¼ tsp. ground black pepper

Time: 8 min. | Servings: 4 | Calories: 195

Directions

Preheat the broiler. Line a baking dish with aluminum foil. Arrange the sardines in a single layer on the foil. Combine the olive oil, garlic, and red pepper flakes in a bowl and spoon over each sardine. Season with salt and pepper. Broil for 2-3 min. Serve, each plate and topped with garlic mixture.

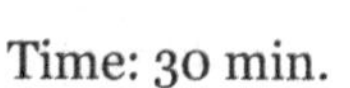

Paprika Crab Burgers

Ingredients

- 2 eggs, beaten
- 1 shallot, chopped
- 2 garlic cloves, crushed
- 1 tbsp. olive oil
- 1 tsp. yellow mustard
- 1 tsp. cilantro, chopped
- 10 oz. crab meat
- 1 tsp. smoked paprika
- ½ tsp. ground black pepper
- Sea salt, to taste
- ¾ cup Parmesan cheese

Time: 44 min. | Servings: 3 | Calories: 288

Directions

In a bowl, mix eggs, shallot, garlic, olive oil, mustard, cilantro, crab meat, paprika, black pepper, and salt until well combined. Shape into 6 patties and coat with grated Parmesan cheese. Refrigerate for 2 hr. Spritz patties with cooking oil on both sides. Cook in a preheated air fryer at 360°F for 14 min. Serve on dinner rolls if desired. Bon appétit!

Tuna Cakes

Ingredients

- 4 (3 oz.) pouches tuna, drained
- 1 large egg, whisked
- 2 tbsp. peeled and chopped white onion
- ½ tsp. Old Bay seasoning

Time: 20 min. | Servings: 4 | Calories: 113

Directions

In a large bowl, mix all ingredients together and form into four patties. Place patties into ungreased air fryer basket. Adjust the temperature to 400°F and air fry for 10 min. Patties will be browned and crispy when done. Let cool 5 min. before serving.

Lemon-Oregano Grilled Shrimp

Ingredients

- ½ cup oregano leaves
- 1 clove garlic, minced
- 1 tsp. grated lemon zest
- 3 tbsp. lemon juice
- ¾ tsp. salt, plus more
- ½ tsp. ground black pepper, plus more
- ½ cup olive oil, plus 2 tbsps., divided
- 2½ Ib. large shrimp, deveined

Time: 16 min. | Servings: 6 | Calories: 389

Directions

In a small bowl, mix oregano, garlic, lemon zest, lemon juice, salt, and pepper. Whisk in ½ cup olive oil. Preheat the grill to high heat. Toss shrimp in the remaining 2 tbsp olive oil and 1-2 tsp salt and pepper. Thread shrimp onto skewers and grill for 2-3 min per side. Transfer skewers to a platter, spoon sauce over them, and serve immediately.

Rainbow Salmon Kebabs

Ingredients

- 6 oz. boneless, skinless salmon, cut into 1-inch cubes
- ¼ medium red onion, peeled and cut into 1-inch pieces
- ½ medium yellow bell pepper, seeded and cut into 1-inch pieces
- ½ medium zucchini, trimmed and cut into ½-inch slices
- 1 tbsp. olive oil
- ½ tsp. salt
- ¼ tsp. ground black pepper

Time: 18 min. | Servings: 2 | Calories: 195

Directions

Using one (6-inch) skewer, 1 piece each of salmon, onion, bell pepper, and zucchini. Repeat this pattern with 4 additional skewers. Drizzle with olive oil and sprinkle with salt and black pepper. Place kebabs into ungreased air fryer basket. Air fry at 400°F for 8 min., turning kebabs halfway through the cook. Serve warm.

Steamed Clams

Ingredients

Time: 18 min. Servings: 4 Calories: 205

- 2 Ib. fresh clams, rinsed
- 1 tbsp. olive oil
- 1 small white onion, diced
- 1 clove garlic, quartered
- ½ cup Chardonnay
- ½ cup water

Directions

Place clams in the Instant Pot basket. Press Sauté and heat oil. Add onion, cook until tender, add garlic and cook for 30 sec. Pour in Chardonnay and water. Insert steamer basket with clams. Press Cancel, close the lid, set steam release to Sealing, press Manual, and set to 4 min. When done, quick-release the pressure. Open lid, transfer clams to bowls, and top with cooking liquid.

Smoked Salmon Crudités

Ingredients

Time: 10 min. Servings: 4 Calories: 92

- 6 oz. smoked wild salmon
- 2 tbsp. roasted garlic aioli
- 1 tbsp. Dijon mustard
- 1 tbsp. chopped scallions, green parts only
- 2 tsp. chopped capers
- ½ tsp. dried dill
- 4 endive spears
- ½ cucumber, cut into ¼-inch-thick rounds

Directions

Roughly chop the smoked salmon and place in a small bowl. Add the aioli, Dijon, scallions, capers, and dill and mix well. Top endive spears and cucumber rounds with a spoonful of smoked salmon mixture and enjoy chilled.

CHAPTER 7: POULTRY AND MEAT

Thyme Chicken with Brussels Sprouts

Ingredients

- 1 tbsp. olive oil
- 2 chicken breasts, skinless, boneless and halved
- 2 cups Brussels sprouts, halved
- 1 cup chicken stock
- 2 thyme springs, chopped
- A pinch of salt and black pepper

Time: 35 min.

Servings: 4

Calories: 240

Directions

Set your Instant Pot to Sauté and heat olive oil. Brown chicken breasts for 5 min. Add the remaining ingredients and whisk. Lock the lid, select Poultry mode, and cook for 20 min at High Pressure. After cooking, do a 10 min natural pressure release, then release any remaining pressure. Open the lid, divide and serve.

Smoky Chicken

Ingredients

- 2 tbsps. smoked paprika
- 2 lbs. chicken breasts

Salt and pepper, to taste

- ½ cup water
- 1 tbsp. olive oil

Time: 20 min.

Servings: 6

Calories: 285

Directions

Sauté olive oil in the Instant Pot. Stir in chicken with paprika and cook for 3 min. Season with salt and pepper, add water. Lock the lid. Cook on Manual for 12 min. at High Pressure. Once complete, do a natural pressure release for 8 min, release any remaining pressure. Garnish with scallions, if desired.

Roasted Red Pepper Chicken

Ingredients

- 1¼ Ib. chicken thighs, pieces
- ½ red onion, cut into chunks
- 2 tbsp. extra-virgin olive oil
- ½ tsp. dried thyme
- ¼ tsp. ground black pepper
- ¼ tsp. kosher or sea salt
- 12 oz. roasted red peppers, chopped
- Lemony Garlic Hummus
- ½ medium lemon
- 3 whole-wheat pita breads, cut into 8

Time: 20 min.

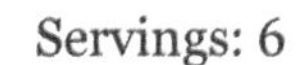

Servings: 6

Calories: 364

Directions

Line a baking sheet with foil. Preheat the broiler to high. Mix chicken, onion, oil, thyme, pepper, and salt in a large bowl. Spread on the sheet and broil for 5 min. Stir in red peppers, broil for another 5 min. Remove from oven. Spread hummus on a platter, top with chicken. Squeeze lemon juice over, and serve with pita.

Lemon Garlic Chicken

Ingredients

- 3 tbsps. olive oil, divided
- 2 tsps. dried parsley
- 6 chicken breasts
- 3 minced garlic cloves
- 1 tbsp. lemon juice
- Salt and pepper, to taste

Time: 32 min.

Servings: 6

Calories: 293

Directions

Mix 2 tbsps. olive oil, chicken, parsley, garlic cloves, and lemon juice in a large bowl. Place in the refrigerator to marinate. Sauté the remaining olive oil in the Instant Pot. Cook the chicken breasts for 5-6 min. per side. Allow to cool for 5 min. before serving.

Baked Teriyaki Turkey Meatballs

Ingredients

- 1 Ib. lean ground turkey
- 1 egg, whisked
- ¼ cup finely chopped scallions
- 2 garlic cloves, minced
- 2 tbsp. reduced-sodium tamari
- 1 tsp. grated fresh ginger
- 1 tbsp. honey
- 2 tsp. mirin
- 1 tsp. olive oil

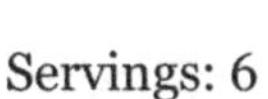

Time: 40 min. Servings: 6 Calories: 158

Directions

Preheat oven to 400°F and line a baking sheet with parchment paper. Mix ground turkey, egg, scallions, garlic, tamari, ginger, honey, mirin, and olive oil in a bowl. Scoop rounded heaps of the mixture, roll into balls, and place on the baking sheet. Bake for 20 min, flipping halfway, until browned and cooked through. Serve warm.

Chicken breast with Olives

Ingredients

- 4 chicken breasts, skinless and boneless
- 2 tbsp. garlic, minced
- 1 tbsp. oregano, dried
- Salt and black pepper to the taste
- 2 tbsp. olive oil
- ½ cup chicken stock
- Juice of 1 lemon
- 1 cup red onion, chopped
- 1 ½ cups tomatoes, cubed
- ¼ cup green olives, sliced
- A handful parsley, chopped

Time: 25 min. Servings: 4 Calories: 135

Directions

Heat up a pan with the oil over medium-high heat, add the chicken, garlic, salt and pepper and brown for 2 min. on each side. Add the rest of the ingredients, toss, bring the mix to a simmer and cook over medium heat for 13 min. Divide the mix between plates and serve.

Beef Spanakopita Pita Pockets

Ingredients

- 3 tsp. extra-virgin olive oil, divided
- 1-Ib. ground beef (93% lean)
- 2 garlic cloves, minced
- 6-oz. baby spinach, chopped
- ½ cup crumbled feta cheese
- ⅓ cup ricotta cheese
- ½ tsp. ground nutmeg
- ¼ tsp. ground black pepper
- ¼ cup slivered almonds
- 4 whole-wheat pita breads, cut in half

Time: 20 min. | Servings: 2 | Calories: 506

Directions

In a skillet, heat oil over medium heat. Add beef and cook for 10 min, stirring occasionally. Drain and set aside. Heat remaining oil in the skillet, add garlic, and cook for 1 min. Add spinach and cook for 2-3 min, stirring often. Turn off heat and mix in feta, ricotta, nutmeg, and pepper. Stir in almonds. Stuff eight pita pockets with beef filling and serve.

Pork Kebabs

Ingredients

- 1 yellow onion, chopped
- 1-Ib. lean pork meat, ground
- 3 tablespoons cilantro, chopped
- 1 tablespoon lime juice
- 1 garlic clove, minced
- 2 teaspoon oregano, dried
- Salt and black pepper to the taste
- A drizzle of olive oil

Time: 20 min. | Servings: 6 | Calories: 229

Directions

In a bowl, mix the pork with the other ingredients except the oil, stir well and shape medium kebabs out of this mix. Divide the kebabs on skewers, and brush them with a drizzle of oil. Place the kebabs on your preheated grill and cook over medium heat for 7 min on each side. Divide the kebabs between plates and serve with a side salad.

Turkey Burgers with Mango Salsa

Ingredients

- 1½ Ib. ground turkey breast
- 1 tsp. sea salt, divided
- ¼ tsp. freshly ground black pepper
- 2 tbsps. extra-virgin olive oil
- 2 mangos, cubed
- ½ red onion, finely chopped
- Juice of 1 lime
- 1 garlic clove, minced
- ½ jalapeño pepper, minced
- 2 tbsp. chopped cilantro

Time: 20 min. 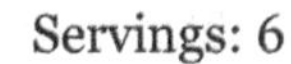 Servings: 6 Calories: 284

Directions

Form 4 turkey patties and season with ½ tsp. sea salt and pepper. Heat olive oil in a non-stick skillet over medium-high heat until shimmering. Cook the patties for 5 min. per side. While they cook, mix mango, red onion, lime juice, garlic, jalapeño, cilantro, and the remaining ½ tsp. sea salt in a bowl. Spoon the salsa over the patties and serve.

Beef & Eggplant Casserole

Ingredients

- 1 eggplant peeled, cut lengthwise
- ½ cup lean ground beef
- 1 onion, chopped
- 1 tsp olive oil
- ¼ tsp. freshly ground black pepper
- 1 tomato
- 2 tbsp. freshly chopped parsley

Time: 25 min. Servings: 2 Calories: 331

Directions

Place eggplants in a bowl and Season with salt. Let sit for 10 min. Rinse and drain. Grease the pot with oil. Stir-fry onions for 2 min. Add beef, tomato, and cook for 5 min. Transfer to a bowl. Make a layer with eggplant in the pot. Spread the beef mix over and sprinkle with parsley. Make another layer with eggplants and repeat. Seal the lid and cook for 12 min. Do a quick release.

Tahini Chicken Rice Bowls

Ingredients

Time: 25 min. | Servings: 4 | Calories: 420

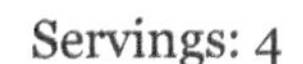

- 1 cup brown rice
- ¼ cup tahini
- ¼ cup Greek yogurt
- 2 tbsp. chopped scallions
- 1 tbsp. squeezed lemon juice
- 1 tsp. ground cumin
- ¾ tsp. ground cinnamon
- ¼ tsp. kosher or sea salt
- 2 cups cooked chicken breast
- ½ cup chopped dried apricots
- 2 cups chopped cucumber
- 4 tsp. sesame seeds
- Optional: Fresh mint leaves

Directions

Cook the brown rice as per the package instructions. In a bowl, combine tahini, yogurt, scallions, lemon juice, water, cumin, cinnamon, and salt. Transfer half of this mix to another bowl and add the chicken. Once the rice is cooked, mix it into the bowl with the chicken. Divide the chicken among 4 bowls. Serve with rice mix, dried apricots, cucumbers, sesame seeds, and mint, if desired.

Easy Turkey Tenderloin

Ingredients

Time: 50 min. | Servings: 4 | Calories: 196

- Olive oil
- ½ teaspoon paprika
- ½ teaspoon garlic powder
- ½ teaspoon salt
- ½ teaspoon freshly ground black pepper
- Pinch cayenne pepper
- 1½ pounds turkey breast tenderloin

Directions

Spray the air fryer basket with olive oil. In a bowl, combine paprika, garlic powder, salt, black pepper, and cayenne pepper. Rub the mix over the turkey. Spray the turkey in the air fryer basket with olive oil. Air fry at 370°F for 15 min. Flip the turkey and spray with olive oil. Air fry at least 170°F for 10 to 15 min. Cool for 10 min. before serving.

Grilled Chicken and Vegetable with Sauce

Ingredients

- 1 cup chopped walnuts, toasted
- 1 shallot, very finely chopped
- ½ cup olive oil
- Juice and zest of 1 lemon
- 4 skinless chicken breasts
- Sea salt and ground pepper
- 2 zucchinis, sliced
- ½ pound asparagus
- 1 onion, sliced ⅓-inch thick
- 1 tsp. Italian seasoning

Time: 36 min.

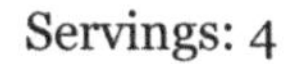
Servings: 4

Calories: 800

Directions

Preheat a grill. Blend walnuts, shallots, olive oil, lemon juice, and zest in a food processor until smooth. Season chicken with salt and pepper, and grill for 7–8 min. When chicken is halfway done, add vegetables. Sprinkle Italian seasoning. To serve, place grilled veggies on a plate, top with chicken, and spoon lemon-walnut sauce over everything.

Spicy Chicken Breasts

Ingredients

- 1 ½ Ib. chicken breasts
- 1 bell pepper, deveined and chopped
- 1 leek, chopped
- 1 tomato, pureed
- 2 tbsp. coriander
- 2 garlic cloves, minced
- 1 tsp. cayenne pepper
- 1 tsp. dry thyme
- ¼ cup coconut amino
- Sea salt
- Ground black pepper

Time: 45 min.

Servings: 6

Calories: 239

Directions

Rub each chicken breasts with garlic, cayenne pepper, thyme, salt, and black pepper. Cook the chicken in a pan over medium-high heat. Sear for about 5 min. on all sides. Add the tomato puree and coconut amino and bring it to a boil. Add in the pepper, leek, and coriander. Simmer and cook, partially covered, for about 20 min.

Chicken with Chickpeas and Sauce

Ingredients

- 2 Ib. boneless, skinless chicken thighs
- Sea salt
- Ground black pepper
- 2 tbsp. olive oil, divided
- 1 onion, chopped
- 3 garlic cloves, minced
- 1 cup chicken broth
- 1 tbsp. harissa sauce
- 15 oz. chickpeas, drained
- ¼ cup chopped parsley

Time: 40 min. Servings: 4 Calories: 552

Directions

Season chicken thighs with salt and pepper. Heat 1 tbsp. olive oil in a skillet over medium-high heat. Cook chicken for 2-3 min per side. Set aside. Heat remaining oil in the same skillet. Sauté onion and garlic for 4-5 min. Return chicken, add broth and sauce. Boil, simmer for 15 min. Add chickpeas, simmer 5 min. Garnish with parsley and serve.

Authentic Turkey Kebabs

Ingredients

- 1 ½ Ib. turkey breast, cubed
- 3 Spanish peppers, sliced
- 2 zucchinis, cut into thick slices
- 1 onion, cut into wedges
- 2 tbsp. olive oil, room temperature
- 1 tbsp. dry ranch seasoning

Time: 35 min. Servings: 6 Calories: 258

Directions

Thread the turkey pieces and vegetables onto bamboo skewers. Sprinkle the skewers with dry ranch seasoning and olive oil. Grill your kebabs for about 10 min., turning them periodically to ensure even cooking. Wrap in foil before packing them into airtight containers; keep them in your refrigerator for up to 3 days

CHAPTER 8: FRUITS AND DESSERT

Italian Chocolate Cake

Ingredients

- 11 tbsp., unsalted butter
- 5 ounces of dark chocolate chips, minimum 70% cacao
- 3 large room-temperature eggs
- ¾ cup of almond flour
- 2/3 cup of granulated sugar
- ¼ tsp of salt
- Confectioners' sugar

Time: 45 min. Servings: 8 Calories: 450

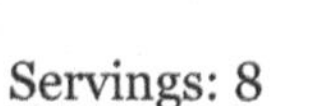

Directions

Preheat oven to 350°F. Oil an 8-10-inch cake tin and line with parchment. Melt chocolate on LOW. Mix sugar, salt, and butter. Add flour and eggs; beat until smooth. Cool chocolate slightly, mix into batter. Pour into tin and bake for 25-30 min. Cool, remove from pan, then dust with confectioner's sugar before serving.

Carrot Cake with Cashew

Ingredients

- 2 cups grated carrots
- 1 cup whole wheat flour
- 1/2 cup olive oil
- 1/2 cup honey
- 1/2 cup cashews, chopped
- 2 eggs
- 1 tsp baking powder
- 1 tsp cinnamon

Time: 50 min. Servings: 8 Calories: 250

Directions

Preheat oven to 350°F. Mix carrots, olive oil, and honey in a bowl. Add eggs and blend well. Combine flour, baking powder, cinnamon, and salt in another bowl. Add dry ingredients to the wet mix. Fold in cashews. Pour into a greased baking dish. Bake for 30 min Allow to cool before serving.

Roasted Orange Rice Pudding

Ingredients

- Nonstick cooking spray
- 2 medium oranges
- 2 tsp extra-virgin olive oil
- ⅛ tsp kosher or sea salt
- 2 large eggs, beaten
- 2 cups 2% milk
- 1 cup orange juice
- 1 cup uncooked instant brown rice
- ¼ cup honey
- ½ tsp ground cinnamon
- 1 tsp vanilla extract

Time: 30 min. | Servings: 6 | Calories: 289

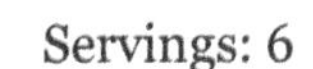

Directions

Preheat the oven to 230°C. Spray a rimmed baking sheet. Slice oranges, brush with oil, sprinkle with salt, and roast for 4 min per side. In a pan, mix milk, juice, rice, honey, and cinnamon. Boil, then simmer for 10 min. Mix ½ cup hot rice with eggs, then stir into the pan. Cook for 1-2 min, remove from heat, and stir in vanilla. Let rest. Serve warm with roasted oranges.

Chocolate Coffee Cake

Ingredients

- 2 cups of all-purpose flour
- 2 cups of white sugar
- ½ cup of unsweetened cocoa powder
- 1 tbsp. of baking powder
- 1 tsp of ground coffee
- 2 cups of plain, full-fat yogurt
- ½ cup of extra virgin olive oil
- 2 eggs
- A pinch of salt

Time: 50 min. | Servings: 8 | Calories: 495

Directions

Preheat your oven to 350°F and brush olive oil over a 10-inch round cake tin. Dust it with flour and set aside. Sift and whisk the dry ingredients. Beat the wet ingredients for one min. Add the dry to the wet, whisking to combine to a silky smooth consistency. Pour the batter into the tin and bake it for 45 to 50 min. Serve with a little plain yogurt.

Banana Oatmeal Cookies

Ingredients

- 1 cup rolled oats
- 1 ripe banana, mashed
- ¼ cup unsweetened applesauce
- ¼ cup chopped nuts (such as almonds or walnuts)
- ¼ cup raisins or dried cranberries
- 1 tsp. cinnamon
- 1/2 tsp. vanilla extract

Time: 25 min. | Servings: 3 | Calories: 70

Directions

Preheat oven to 350°F and line a baking sheet with parchment. Mix oats, mashed banana, applesauce, nuts, raisins, cinnamon, and vanilla. Shape into cookies and flatten slightly. Bake for 12-15 min until golden. Cool on the sheet briefly, then transfer to a wire rack to cool completely.

Yogurt Parfait with Granola

Ingredients

- 1 cup Greek yogurt
- 1/2 cup granola
- 1/2 cup pomegranate seeds
- 1 tablespoon honey (optional)
- A pinch of cinnamon (optional)

Time: 10 min. | Servings: 2 | Calories: 250

Directions

Divide the Greek yogurt between two glasses or bowls. Layer each with granola and pomegranate seeds. Drizzle honey over each parfait and sprinkle with a pinch of cinnamon if desired. Serve immediately or chill until ready to serve

Almond Coconut Energy Bites

Ingredients

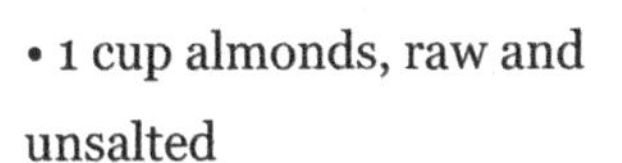

- 1 cup almonds, raw and unsalted
- 1 cup shredded coconut, unsweetened
- 1/4 cup almond butter
- 1/4 cup honey or maple syrup
- 1 tsp. vanilla extract
- Pinch of salt

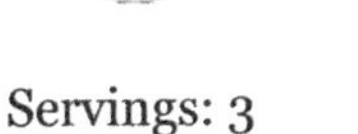

Time: 15 min. | Servings: 3 | Calories: 170

Directions

Pulse almonds in a food processor until finely chopped. Add shredded coconut, almond butter, honey/maple syrup, vanilla extract, and a pinch of salt. Pulse until a sticky dough forms. Roll into bite-sized balls, place on a parchment-lined sheet, and refrigerate for 30 min. Store in an airtight container.

Cinnamon Banana and Semolina Pudding

Ingredients

- 2 cups semolina, ground
- 1 cup olive oil
- 4 cups hot water
- 2 bananas, peeled and chopped
- 1 teaspoon cinnamon powder
- 4 tablespoons stevia

Time: 7 min. | Servings: 6 | Calories: 162

Directions

Heat up a pan with the oil over medium high heat, add the semolina and brown it for 3 minutes stirring often. Add the water and the rest of the ingredients except the cinnamon, stir, and simmer for 4 minutes more. Divide into bowls, sprinkle the cinnamon on top and serve.

Baked Apples with Walnuts and Spices

Ingredients

Time: 15 min. | Servings: 3 | Calories: 170

- 4 apples
- ¼ cup chopped walnuts
- 2 tablespoons honey
- 1 teaspoon ground cinnamon
- ¼ teaspoon ground nutmeg
- ¼ teaspoon ground ginger
- Pinch sea salt

Directions

Preheat the oven to 375°F. Cut the apples tops and remove the cores, leaving the bottoms of the apples intact. Place the cut-side up in a 9-by-9-inch baking pan. In a bowl, stir the walnuts, honey, cinnamon, nutmeg, ginger, and sea salt. Pour into the centers of the apples. Bake the apples for about 45 minutes until browned, soft, and fragrant. Serve warm.

Vanilla Greek Yogurt Affogato

Ingredients

Time: 10 min. | Servings: 4 | Calories: 157

- 24 ounces' vanilla Greek yogurt
- 2 teaspoons sugar
- ¾ cup (6 ounces) strong brewed coffee
- 4 tablespoons chopped unsalted pistachios
- 4 tablespoons dark chocolate chips or shavings

Directions

Spoon the yogurt into four bowls or tall glasses. Mix ½ tsp of sugar into each of the espresso shots (or all the sugar into the coffee). Pour one shot of hot espresso or 1.5 ounces of coffee over each bowl of yogurt. Top each bowl with 1 tbsp. of pistachios and 1 tbsp. of chocolate chips and serve.

Almond Pudding

Ingredients

- ½ cup organic almond milk
- ½ cup milk
- 1/3 cup semolina
- 1 tablespoon butter
- ¼ teaspoon corn-starch
- ½ teaspoon almond extract

Time: 22 min. Servings: 3 Calories: 208

Directions

Pour almond milk and milk into the saucepan. Bring it to a boil and add semolina and corn starch. Mix the until homogenous and simmer them for 1 minute. After this, add almond extract and butter. Stir well and close the lid. After 10 min, switch off the heat and let the pudding cool. Then mix it up again and transfer it to the serving ramekins.

Blackberry and Apples Cobbler

Ingredients

- ¼ cup apples, cored and cubed
- ¼ teaspoon baking powder
- ½ cup almond flour
- ½ cup water
- ¾ cup stevia
- 1 tablespoon lime juice
- 3 ½ tablespoon avocado oil cooking spray
- 6 cups blackberries

Time: 40 min. Servings: 6 Calories: 190

Directions

Mix berries with half the stevia and lemon juice in a bowl. Add flour, beat, and pour into a greased baking dish. In another bowl, combine remaining stevia, baking powder, water, oil, and flour, mixing by hand. Spread over berries, then bake for 30 min at 190°C. Serve warm.

Avocado Chocolate Mousse

Ingredients

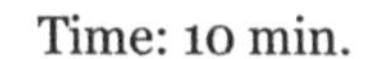

Time: 10 min. Servings: 4 Calories: 170

- 1 Ib. dairy-free dark chocolate
- 1¼ cups unsweetened almond milk
- 4 small ripe avocados—pitted, peeled and chopped
- 1 tbsp. finely grated orange zest
- ¼ cup agave syrup
- 2 tbsp. puffed quinoa
- 2 tsp. Aleppo pepper flakes
- 2 tsp. sea salt
- 1 tbsp. extra-virgin olive oil

Directions

Heat the almond milk in a pan over heat until 175°F. Chop the chocolate, remove from the fire, and mix until smooth. Allow to cool. Blend avocados, agave, orange zest, and chocolate in a blender until smooth. Distribute the mousse among four bowls for serving. Puffed quinoa, sea salt, Aleppo pepper, and olive oil should all be uniformly distributed.

Red Wine Poached Pears

Ingredients

Time: 45 min. Servings: 4 Calories: 248

- 2 cups dry red wine
- ¼ cup honey
- Zest of ½ orange
- 2 cinnamon sticks
- 1 (1-inch) piece fresh ginger
- 4 pears, bottom inch sliced off so the pear is flat

Directions

In a pot over heat, Mix wine, honey, orange zest, cinnamon, and ginger. Boil, stirring occasionally. Reduce heat, simmer for 5 min. Add pears, cover, and simmer for 20 min, turn every 3-4 min. chill in liquid for 3 hours. Bring to room temp. Simmer liquid over medium-high heat for 15 min until syrupy. Serve pears with syrup drizzled on top.

CHAPTER 9: SAUCE, DIP AND DRESSING

Artichoke and Spinach Dip

Ingredients

- 8 oz. cream cheese, softened
- ½ cup mayonnaise
- ¼ cup Parmesan cheese
- ¼ cup mozzarella cheese
- 1 clove garlic, minced
- ½ tsp. dried basil
- ½ tsp. dried oregano
- ½ tsp. dried thyme
- ½ cup chopped spinach
- ½ cup chopped artichoke
- Salt and pepper to taste

Time: 30 min. | Servings: 4 | Calories: 270

Directions

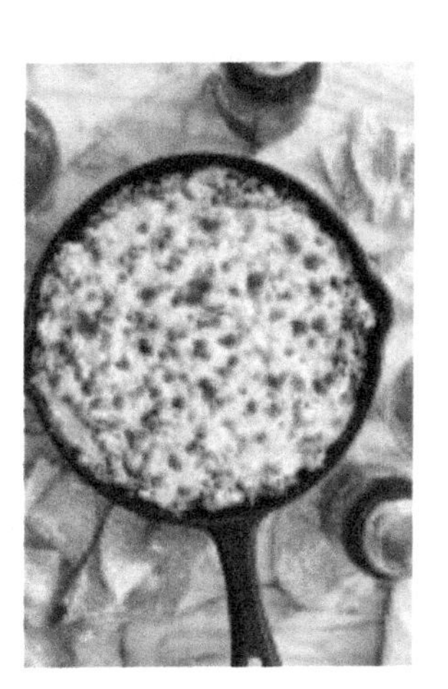

Preheat the oven to 350°F. Mix softened cream cheese, mayonnaise, Parmesan, mozzarella, garlic, basil, oregano, and thyme in a bowl. Stir in spinach and artichoke hearts. Season with salt and pepper. Transfer to a dish, smooth the top, and bake for 20 min until golden. Cool briefly before serving.

White Bean Dip with Garlic and Herbs

Ingredients

- 1 cup dried white beans
- 3 cloves garlic, crushed
- 8 cups water
- ¼ cup extra-virgin olive oil
- ¼ cup chopped parsley
- 1 tbsp. chopped fresh oregano
- 1 tbsp. chopped fresh tarragon
- 1 tsp. chopped thyme leaves
- 1 tsp. grated lemon zest
- ¼ tsp. salt
- ¼ tsp. ground black pepper

Time: 40 min. | Servings: 16 | Calories: 147

Directions

Place beans and garlic in the Instant Pot and stir. Add water, close lid, select Sealing, press Manual, and set time to 30 min. When it beeps, do a natural release, about 20 min. Open lid, drain off water, and transfer to a processor with oil. Pulse until smooth. Add the remaining ingredients and pulse 3–5 times to mix. Serve cold or at room temperature.

Chickpea, Parsley, and Dill Dip

Ingredients

Time: 26 min. Servings: 2 Calories: 79

- 8 cups plus 2 tbsp. water, divided
- 1 cup dried chickpeas
- 3 tbsp. olive oil, divided
- 2 garlic cloves, peeled and minced
- 2 tbsp. chopped fresh parsley
- 2 tbsp. chopped fresh dill
- 1 tbsp. lemon juice
- ¼ tsp. salt

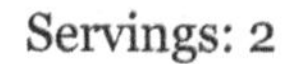

Directions

Add 4 cups water and chickpeas to the Instant Pot. Close lid, select Sealing, Manual, and set for 1 min. Quick-release when it beeps. Drain, rinse, and soak chickpeas in 4 cups fresh water. Add 1 tbsp oil, cook for 20 min, natural release, blend with remaining ingredients, and serve warm.

Black Bean Corn Dip

Ingredients

Time: 20 min. Servings: 4 Calories: 119

- ½ can black beans, drained and rinsed
- ½ can corn, drained and rinsed
- ¼ cup chunky salsa
- 2 oz. cream cheese, softened
- ¼ cup shredded Cheddar cheese
- ½ tsp. ground cumin
- ½ tsp. paprika
- Salt as required

Directions

Preheat the air fryer to 325°F. In a medium bowl, mix together the black beans, corn, salsa, cream cheese, Cheddar cheese, cumin, and paprika. Season with salt and pepper and stir until well combined. Spoon the mixture into a baking dish. Place baking dish in the air fryer basket and bake until heated through, about 10 minutes. Serve hot.

Hummus

Ingredients

- 1 can chickpeas, drained and rinsed
- 1/4 cup tahini
- 2 tbsp. olive oil
- 2 cloves garlic, minced
- 1 lemon, juiced
- 1/2 teaspoon ground cumin
- Salt and pepper to taste
- 1/4 cup water (as needed for consistency)

Time: 5 min. Servings: 1 Calories: 140

Directions

In a food processor, combine the chickpeas, tahini, olive oil, minced garlic, lemon juice, ground cumin, salt, and pepper. Blend until smooth, adding water as needed to reach desired consistency. How to Serve: Serve as a dip with pita bread or fresh vegetables, or as a spread for sandwiches.

Piri Piri Sauce

Ingredients

- 4 to 8 fresh hot, red chills, stemmed and coarsely chopped
- 2 cloves garlic, minced
- Juice of 1 lemon
- Pinch of salt
- ½ to 1 cup olive oil

Time: 5 min. Servings: 1 Calories: 84

Directions

In a food processor, combine the chills, garlic, lemon juice, salt, and ½ cup of oil. Process to a smooth purée. Add extra oil as needed to reach the desired consistency. Pour the mix into a jar or non-reactive bowl, cover, and refrigerate for at least 3 days before using. Store in the refrigerator for up to a month.

Pesto Sauce

Ingredients

Time: 5 min. | Servings: 1 | Calories: 180

- 2 cups fresh basil leaves
- 1/2 cup Parmesan cheese, grated
- 1/2 cup pine nuts
- 2 cloves garlic, minced
- 1/2 cup olive oil
- Salt and pepper to taste

Directions

In a food processor, combine the basil leaves, Parmesan cheese, pine nuts, and minced garlic. Blend until the ingredients are finely chopped. With the food processor running, slowly drizzle in the olive oil until the mixture is smooth. Season with salt and pepper to taste. Serve as a sauce for pasta, a spread for sandwiches, or a dip for bread.

Tzatziki Sauce

Ingredients

Time: 5 min. | Servings: 2 | Calories: 80

- 1 cup Greek yogurt
- 1 cucumber, grated and excess water squeezed out
- 2 cloves garlic, minced
- 1 tbsp. fresh dill, chopped
- 1 tbsp. fresh mint, chopped
- 1 tbsp. olive oil
- 1 tbsp. lemon juice
- Salt and pepper to taste

Directions

In a medium bowl, combine the Greek yogurt, grated cucumber, minced garlic, dill, mint, olive oil, lemon juice, salt, and pepper. Mix well until all ingredients are evenly distributed. Serve chilled as a dip with pita bread or fresh vegetables, or as a sauce for grilled meats.

Romesco Sauce

Ingredients

- 2 roasted red bell peppers, peeled and seeded
- 1/2 cup almonds, toasted
- 2 cloves garlic, minced
- 1/4 cup olive oil
- 2 tbsp. red wine vinegar
- 1 tsp. smoked paprika
- Salt and pepper to taste

Time: 5 min. | Servings: 1 | Calories: 120

Directions

In a food processor, combine the roasted red bell peppers, toasted almonds, minced garlic, olive oil, red wine vinegar, and smoked paprika. Blend until smooth. Season with salt and pepper to taste. Serve as a dip with vegetables or bread, or as a sauce for grilled meats or seafood

Salsa Verde

Ingredients

- 4 cups fresh parsley leaves
- 8 garlic cloves, minced
- ¼ tsp. table salt
- ¼ cup sherry vinegar
- 1 cup extra-virgin olive oil

Time: 5 min. | Servings: 2 | Calories: 341

Directions

Pulse parsley, garlic, and salt in food processor until parsley is coarsely chopped, about 10 pulses. Add vinegar and pulse briefly to combine. Transfer mixture to bowl and whisk in oil until incorporated. Cover and let sit at room temperature for 30 min to allow flavors to meld. Sauce can be refrigerated for up to 2 days; serve warm..

Traditional Caesar Dressing

Ingredients

- 2 tsp. minced garlic
- 4 large egg yolks
- 1/4 cup wine vinegar
- 1/2 tsp. dry mustard
- Dash Worcestershire sauce
- 1 cup extra-virgin olive oil
- 1/4 cup freshly squeezed lemon juice
- Sea salt and ground black pepper, to taste

Time: 15 min.

Servings: 1

Calories: 202

Directions

Add garlic, egg yolks, vinegar, mustard, and sauce to a saucepan over low heat. Whisk constantly until thick and bubbly, about 5 min. Remove from heat and cool for 10 min. Transfer to a bowl, whisking in olive oil in a thin stream. Add lemon juice, salt, and pepper. Store in an airtight container in the fridge. Serve warm.

Lemon Tahini Dressing

Ingredients

- 1/4 cup tahini
- 3 tbsp. lemon juice
- 3 tbsp. warm water
- 1/4 tsp. kosher salt
- 1/4 tsp. pure maple syrup
- 1/4 tsp. ground cumin
- 1/8 tsp. cayenne pepper

Time: 5 min.

Servings: 1

Calories: 90

Directions

In a medium bowl, whisk together the tahini, lemon juice, water, salt, maple syrup, cumin, and cayenne pepper until smooth. Place in the refrigerator until ready to serve. Store any leftovers in the refrigerator in an airtight container up to 5 days.

Sun-Dried Tomato and Mushroom Dressing

Ingredients

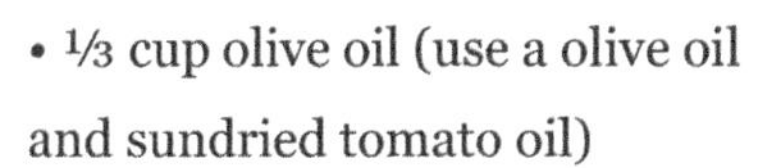

- ⅓ cup olive oil (use a olive oil and sundried tomato oil)
- 8 oz. mushrooms, sliced
- 3 tbsp. red wine vinegar
- Freshly ground black pepper, to taste
- ½ cup sun-dried tomatoes, drained (if they are packed in oil, reserve the oil) and chopped

Time: 27 min. | Servings: 3 | Calories: 363

Directions

In a medium skillet, heat 2 tablespoons of the olive oil (or mixed olive oil and sun-dried tomato packing oil) over high heat. Add the mushrooms and cook, stirring, until they have released their liquid. Add vinegar and season with pepper. Remove from the heat and add the remaining oil and the sun-dried tomatoes.

Creamy Grapefruit-Tarragon Dressing

Ingredients

- ½ cup avocado oil mayonnaise
- 2 tbsp. Dijon mustard
- 1 tsp. dried tarragon or 1 tbsp. chopped fresh tarragon
- Zest and juice of ½ grapefruit (about 2 tbsp. juice)
- ½ tsp. salt
- ¼ tsp. freshly ground black pepper
- 1 to 2 tbsp. water (optional)

Time: 5 min. | Servings: 4-6 | Calories: 49

Directions

In a large mason jar or glass measuring cup, combine the mayonnaise, Dijon, tarragon, grapefruit zest and juice, salt, and pepper and whisk well with a fork until smooth and creamy. If a thinner dressing is preferred, thin out with water.

CONCLUSION

Many struggles to stay healthy, especially when it comes to our diet. With quick, convenient food options available at every corner, it becomes easy to resort to unhealthy meals. While these options may provide temporary satisfaction, they often leave us unfulfilled in the long run. Unfortunately, many fall into unhealthy eating patterns, which when combined with our lifestyle, contribute to a range of serious health issues. As a result, life expectancy is decreasing, and many find themselves dealing with health problems that could have been avoided with better dietary choices.

However, it's never too late to make a positive change. To break free from unhealthy habits, adopt Mediterranean diet that promotes long-term health. It is a lifestyle that emphasizes fresh, seasonal ingredients and a balanced approach to nutrition. For centuries, people living in Mediterranean regions have thrived on diets rich in vegetables, fruits, whole grains, lean proteins, and healthy fats like olive oil. This way of eating has been proven to enhance and promote the health lifestyle of the people of the region.

The diet is renowned for its health benefits, including improved heart health, boosted brain health, facilitated weight loss, and prevented chronic diseases. Imagine you embrace such a diet, it will surely nourish your body and lead to a more balanced, fulfilling life! This concept is no longer a fantasy but a reality, the book demystifies the Mediterranean diet fundamentals, making it accessible for Beginners and pros alike.

Yet, despite the growing interest in the Mediterranean diet, many people struggle with how to incorporate it into their daily routine. With so much conflicting information out there about diets and healthy eating, it's easy to feel overwhelmed. The good news is that adopting the Mediterranean way of eating is not only possible but also enjoyable and deeply satisfying.

Therefore, this cookbook is designed to make the transition to Mediterranean diet simple and stress-free. The recipes in this book are straightforward, focusing on wholesome ingredients and easy-to-follow techniques. They are not only healthy and nutritious but are also uniquely photographed which make them visually appealing. Furthermore, they are user-friendly, painstakingly guides you, step by step, to achieve the perfect dish. The, flavors also add special touches that will impress you while aiding your diet journey.

The recipes photos aren't just appealing; they are visual inspirations that bring the recipes to life. This book has given you the knowledge to transform your health and enrich your life. Thus, the journey doesn't have to end here. Share your experience and favorite recipes from this book with your family and friends. Healthy living is communal, so why not spread the benefits far and wide? If you've enjoyed Mediterranean Diet for Beginners don't forget to leave a feedback to help others know better about the diet. Remember, this lifestyle is gradual process towards a healthy, fulfilling life. So, to get used to it concepts, revisit this book whenever you need fresh ideas or want to relive the joy of cooking healthful, delicious meals.

Made in the USA
Coppell, TX
04 October 2024

38160881R00044